Street by Street

CHESTER

BUCKLEY, CONNAH'S QUAY, FLINT, MOLD, QUEENSFERRY

Bagillt, Blacon, Broughton, Christleton, Ewloe, Greenfield, Hawarden, Higher Kinnerton, Holywell, Hope, Mickle Trafford, Northop, Penyffordd, Saltney, Saughall, Soughton

3rd edition May 2008
© Automobile Association Developments Limited 2008

Original edition printed May 2001

 This product includes map data licensed from Ordnance Survey® with the permission of the Controller of Her Majesty's Stationery Office. © Crown copyright 2008. All rights reserved. Licence number 100021153.

The copyright in all PAF is owned by Royal Mail Group plc.

Published by AA Publishing (a trading name of Automobile Association Developments Limited, whose registered office is Fanum House, Basing View, Basingstoke, Hampshire RG21 4EA. Registered number 1878835).

Produced by the Mapping Services Department of The Automobile Association. (A03620)

A CIP Catalogue record for this book is available from the British Library.

Printed by Oriental Press in Dubai

Ref: ML081y

Key to map pages	ii-iii
Key to map symbols	iv-1
Enlarged map pages	2-3
Main map pages	4-51
Index – towns & villages	52
Index – streets	52-58
Index – featured places	58-59
Acknowledgements	59

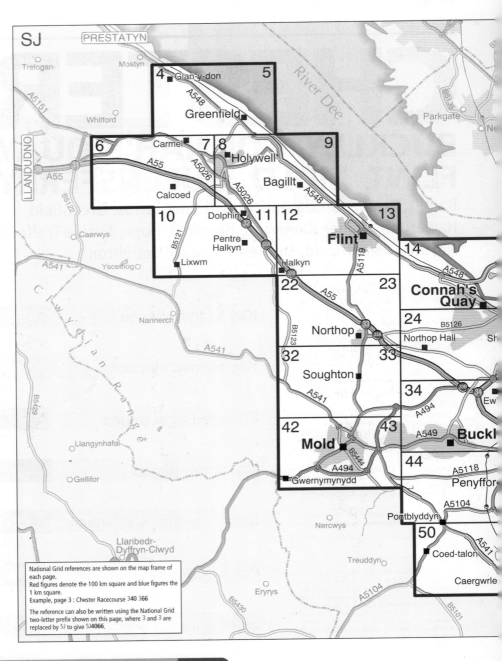

SJ · PRESTATYN

Trelogan · Mostyn · Whitford · LLANDUDNO · Caerwys · Ysceifiog · Nannerch · Llangynhafal · Gellifor · Llanbedr-Dyffryn-Clwyd

River Dee · Parkgate · Ne

4 · Glan-y-don · 5 · A548
6 · Carmel · 7 · 8 · Holywell · 9 · Greenfield · A55 · A5026 · Calcoed · Bagillt · A548
10 · Dolphin · 11 · 12 · Flint · 13 · Pentre Halkyn · Lixwm · Halkyn · 14 · A5119 · Connah's Quay
22 · 23 · Northop · A55 · B5123 · 24 · B5126 · Northop Hall · Sh
32 · 33 · Soughton · A541 · 34 · A494 · Ew
42 · Mold · 43 · B5444 · A549 · Buckl · 44 · A5118 · Penyffor
A494 · Gwernymynydd · A5104 · Pontblyddyn · Penyffor · 50 · Coed-talon · A541 · Caergwrle

Nercwys · Treuddyn · Eryrys · Llanbedr-Dyffryn-Clwyd

B5122 · A5151 · A541 · B5429 · B5430 · B5101 · B5121 · A5026 · A5104 · A548 · B5135

National Grid references are shown on the map frame of each page.
Red figures denote the 100 km square and blue figures the 1 km square.
Example, page 3 : Chester Racecourse 340 366

The reference can also be written using the National Grid two-letter prefix shown on this page, where 3 and 3 are replaced by SJ to give SJ4066.

Scale of enlarged map pages 1:10,000 · 6.3 inches to 1 mile

0 · 1/4 · miles · 1/2
0 · 1/4 · 1/2 · kilometres · 3/4 · 1

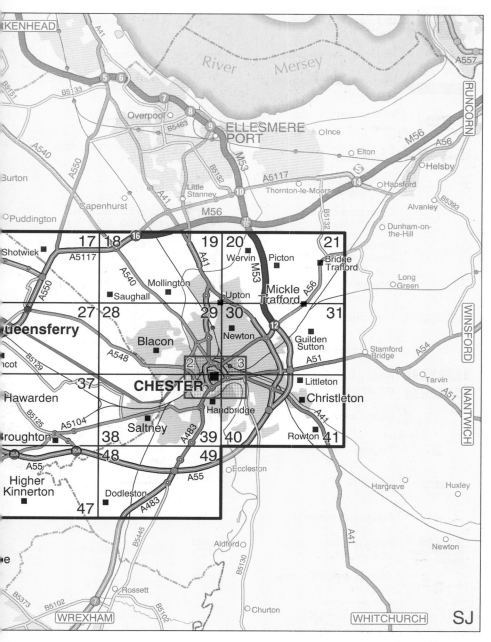

3.6 inches to 1 mile | **Scale of main map pages** | **1:17,500**

iv

Junction 9	Motorway & junction
Services	Motorway service area
	Primary road single/dual carriageway
Services	Primary road service area
	A road single/dual carriageway
	B road single/dual carriageway
	Other road single/dual carriageway
	Minor/private road, access may be restricted
← ←	One-way street
	Pedestrian area
	Track or footpath
	Road under construction
	Road tunnel
P	Parking
P+	Park & Ride
	Bus/coach station
	Railway & main railway station
	Railway & minor railway station
⊖	Underground station
⊖	Light railway & station
	Preserved private railway

LC	Level crossing
	Tramway
	Ferry route
	Airport runway
	County, administrative boundary
	Mounds
17	Page continuation 1:17,500
3	Page continuation to enlarged scale 1:10,000
	River/canal, lake, pier
	Aqueduct, lock, weir
465 ▲ Winter Hill	Peak (with height in metres)
	Beach
	Woodland
	Park
	Cemetery
	Built-up area
	Industrial building
	Leisure building
	Retail building
	Other building

ⴄⴄⴄⴄⴄⴄ	City wall		♜	Castle
A&E	Hospital with 24-hour A&E department		⌸	Historic house or building
PO	Post Office		Wakehurst Place (NT)	National Trust property
📖	Public library		Ⓜ	Museum or art gallery
ℹ	Tourist Information Centre		♞	Roman antiquity
ℹ	Seasonal Tourist Information Centre		⚱	Ancient site, battlefield or monument
▮ ▮	Petrol station, 24 hour Major suppliers only		⛭	Industrial interest
†	Church/chapel		✿	Garden
🚻	Public toilets		◉	Garden Centre Garden Centre Association Member
♿	Toilet with disabled facilities		♣	Garden Centre Wyevale Garden Centre
PH	Public house AA recommended		♣♣	Arboretum
❶	Restaurant AA inspected		🛒	Farm or animal centre
Madeira Hotel	Hotel AA inspected		🦌	Zoological or wildlife collection
🎭	Theatre or performing arts centre		🦜	Bird collection
🎥	Cinema		🦆	Nature reserve
⚑	Golf course		🐟	Aquarium
▲	Camping AA inspected		Ⅴ	Visitor or heritage centre
⛺	Caravan site AA inspected		♆	Country park
▲⛟	Camping & caravan site AA inspected		⌒	Cave
🎢	Theme park		✗	Windmill
🏛	Abbey, cathedral or priory		🛢	Distillery, brewery or vineyard

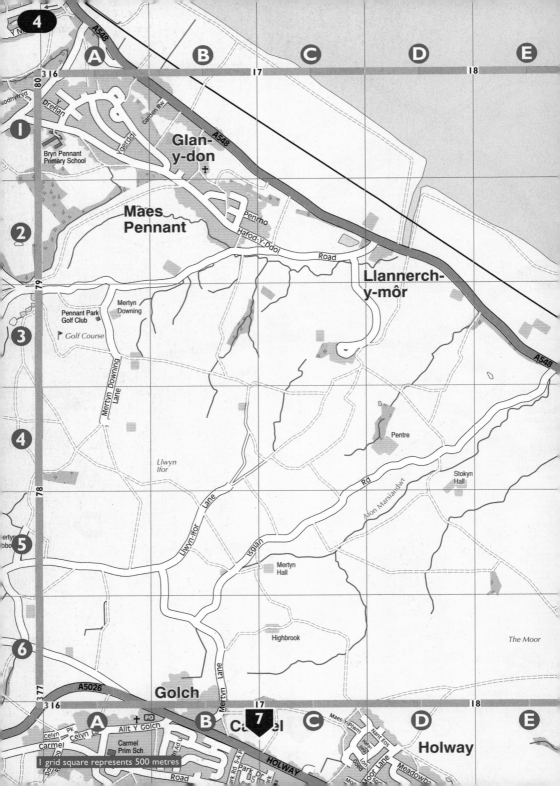

4

A B C D E

17   18

Y Drefian

Bryn Pennant
Primary School

Garden RW

**Glan-
y-don**

A548

**Maes
Pennant**

Penrho

Hafod-Y-Ddol

Road

**Llannerch-
y-môr**

80 316

79

I

2

Mertyn
Downing

Pennant Park
Golf Club

Golf Course

3

Mertyn Downing Lane

4

*Llwyn
Ifor*

Pentre

Stokyn
Hall

78

Llwyn Ifor Lane

Rd

Afon Marsiandwr

5

Mertyn
Hall

Isglan

6

Highbrook

The Moor

A5026

Golch

Mertyn Lane

316   18

377

A B C D E

7

Celyn Pk

Celyn

Carmel

Allt Y Golch

PO

Carmel
Prim Sch

Carmel

Maes Y Plwm

Nant Eos

Holway

HOLWAY

Park Dr

Road

Moor Lane

Meadowbr

I grid square represents 500 metres

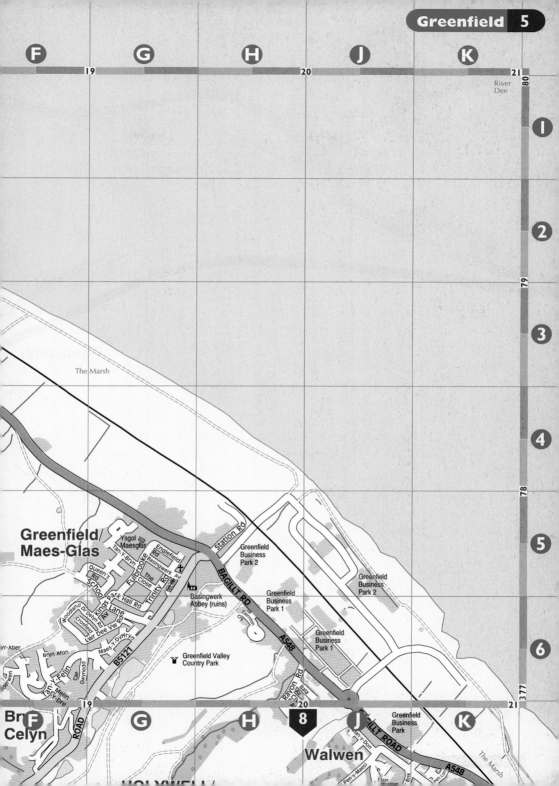

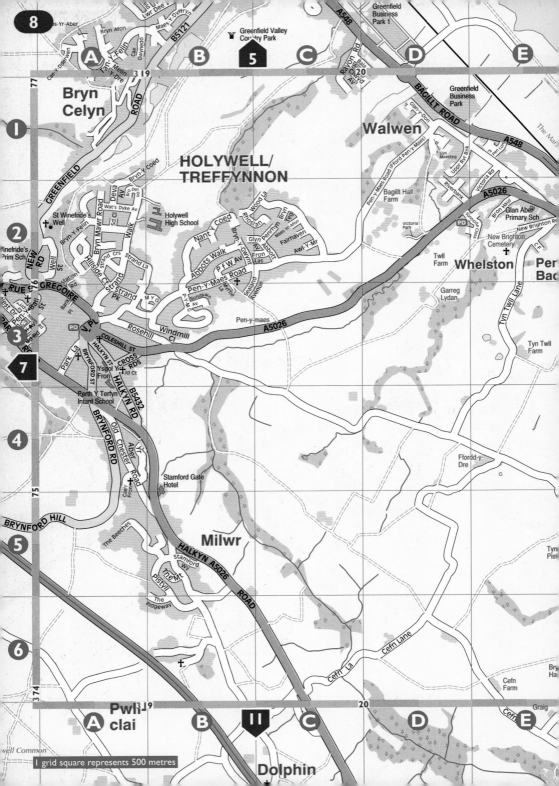

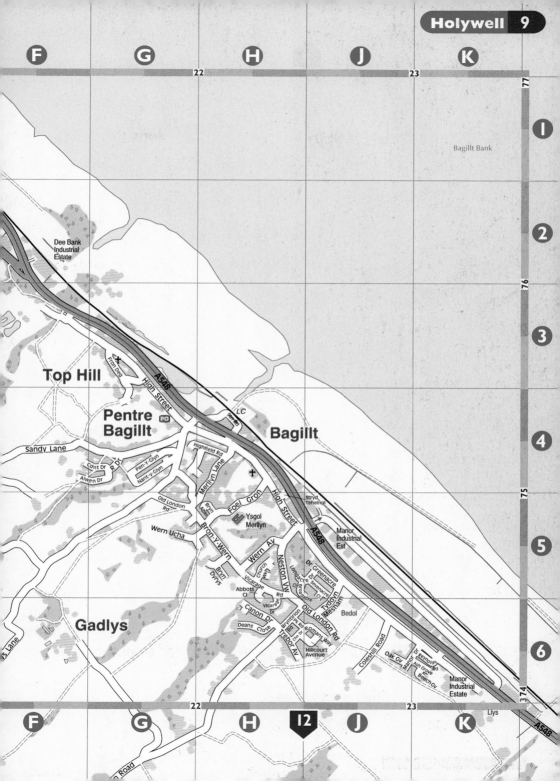

F G H J K

22 23

77

I

Bagillt Bank

2

76

3

Dee Bank
Industrial
Estate

Top Hill

X

Fron Deg

High Street

A548

LC

4

**Pentre
Bagillt**

PO

Bagillt

75

Sandy Lane

Highfield Rd

Merllyn Lane

X

Stryd Teneingl

Cont Dr

Pen-Y-Glyn

Nant-y-Glyn

Alwen Dr

Foel Gron

High Street

A548

Manor
Industrial
Est

5

Old London
Rd

Bryn Adda

Bron-Y-Wern

Ysgol
Merllyn

Wern Ucha

Wern Av

Neston Vw

Dr Greenacre

Longacre

Broadacre

Dr Sevenacres

Gadlys

Bryn
Dyfrs

Church
Av

Vicarage
Rd

Abbots
Cl

Vicarage
Rd

Canon Dr

Deans Close

Brynmor
PK Rd

Q Ohang Way

Old London Rd

Tydalyn
Mesham

Bedol

6

Treflor Av

Hillcourt
Avenue

Coleshill Road

Oak GV

Manor

Dr Reynolds Rd

Ash Grove

Beech Gv

Manor
Industrial
Estate

3 74

Llys

F G H J K

22 23

12

A548

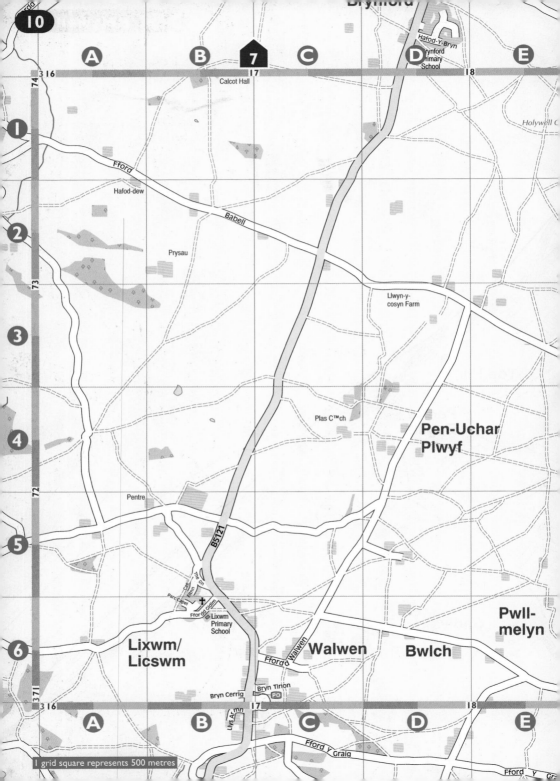

Pwll-clai

Dolphin

Bryn Mawr

Pen yr Henblas

Caeau

Brynford

Llys Dedwydd

Ms Gr

Road

Cae Helyg

Caer Onnen

Bryn Melin

Bryn Allt-y-Plas

Ms Ln

Cae Masarn

Bryn-Y-Mr

Bryn Eithin

PO

Pentre Halkyn

Buxton Lane

Billins

Rhesycae Primary School

Rhes-y-Cae

Trem-y-Foel

Windmill

Hafod Dr

Foel Trwysog

Lon-y-Fron

Bryn y Gwynt

Llys-y-Nant

Fron

Old Hall

Catch

Cefn Lane

Cefn Farm

Bryn Madyn Hall

Gadlys Lan

Graig

Cefn Lane

Llongley

Lygan-y-wern

Bryngwyn

Pistyll

Hafod

B5123

J32

J32a

PENTRE ROAD

A5026

A55

F **G** **H** **8** **J** **K**

19 20 21

74

I

73

2

3

12

4

72

5

6

371

F **G** **H** **J** **K**

19 20 21

14

A   B   C   D   E

White
Sands

I

72

13

2

ROAD

A548

Leadbrook Dr

3

Old Paper Mill Lane

Paper Mill Lane

CHESTER RD

Oakenholt

Rockliffe Lane

Kelsterton Road

Leadbrook
Hall

71

Rockliffe
La

4

Oakenholt Lane

KELSTERTON ROAD

Perenna Ct

Kelsterton Rd

B5129

Deeside
College

Deeside
Stadium

Bad Brook

Connah's Quay
Sports Centre

Golftyn Lane

5

Kelsterton
Lane

Cheshire
Farm

Kelsterton

Connah's Quay
High School

Golftyn Drive

College

Farm

VW

23

3 70

KC

Hatod Cres

Hafod Cl

Golftyn Drive

6

Top-y-
fron

Courter Drive

Degas Cl

Pembry Rise

Monks

Bollam

Millalt

Highmere Drive

Undale

Paynton

Plas
Beilin

A   B   24   C   D   E

W
ddu

Bryn
Saer

Golftyn Lane

Highvale

Higher

F   G   H   J   K

29   30   31

I

WEIGHBRIDGE

72

2

Weighbridge Road

Weighbridge Road

Works

3

16

71

4

North Road

Ring Road

Deeside College
Corus Learning
Centre

Steel Works

Coatings
River

Two

Road

370

5

Golftyn

6

River Dee

Hawarden
Bridge Stati

PO

Dee Vw Rd

Surg

CHURCH HILL

Leighton Ct

Road

Quay Dock

Garthorpe Av

Tuscan

Cable
Way

Cemetery

Bryn Deva
Primary School

**CONNAH'S
QUAY**

Road

HIGH STREET B5129

Chapel St

Prince's
Street

Primrose
Street

Dodd's Drive

Pennant

Surgery

Primary
School

Surgery

Hawarden
Bridge

Shotton

F   G   H   J   K

29 St David's Drive   30   25   31

England   Avenue   Pinewood   Avenue

A   B   C   D   E

331   32   33

1

ROAD

A548

72

2

SHOTWICK   ROAD

Cheshire County
Flintshire

S

3

Tenth Av

Tenth Avenue

15

71

Parkway

A548

4

Second Av

Parkway

First

Avenue

Drive A

Drive B

Fourth

Avenue

Parkway
Business
Cen

Drive

First

5

370

Sixth Av

Third Av

Avenue

Drive D

Deeside
Industrial
Estate

Parkway

6

Deva
Business
Park

Hawarden
Bridge Station

Garden City
Industrial Estate

WELSH ROAD

B5441

A550

331   32   33

A   B   26   C   D   E

Hawarden
Bridge

Garden
City

Sealand Avenue

Brookside

Sandy La

wood

AV

Queen's

Kingsle
Road

Brookside
Road

Dee
RD

Sealand Child
Health Centre

Hawthorn VW

Cedar AV

The Gateway
To-Wales Hotel

Sealand

CH5

1 grid square represents 500 metres

otton

Woodbank

WELSH ROAD

F **G** **H** **J** **K**

34 35 36

Shotwick
Dale

I

Woodbank Lane

A550

Shotwick Lane

New
Covert

72

2

A5117

Green La (West)

Shotwicklodge
Farm

Council
Building

3

18

71

Castle
Farm

4

Green

Lane

Saughall Tho
Wedge CE J

Shotwick
House

5

Surgery

East

Alder

Road

370

Surgery

Fox Lea

Crofters Wy

Pentre Ct

6

34 35 36

F **G** **H** **27** **J** **K**

Seahill

Seahill
Farm

Station Ap

Willow
Farm

Green La

Wimbolds
Trafford

F **G** **H** **J** **K**

44 45 46

I

72

2

Morley
Bridge

CHESTER ROAD

A56

3

Bridge
Trafford

Hassals
Lane

71

4

INCE LANE B5132

Park
Farm

Mill Brook

Manor
Farm

5

Plemstall

370

WARRINGTON ROAD

Picton Lane

Plemstall Lane

LC

Holme Farm

6

Street

Dee Road

The York Dr

Cowy Rd

Dante Cl

Glyn Rd

Weaver Gr

Glebe
Mdw

Linda Cl

Plemstall Wy

Plemstall
End

Reece
Close

York
Dr

Wells Cl

Holly Close

Money

Cemetery

Village
School PO

School Lane

Springfields

Carlton
Close

Manor
Farm Close

Grindley
Bank Close

Plemstall
Court

Waxyde
Court

St Peters
Way

Thomas
Cl

Mickle
Trafford

F **G** **H** **J** **K**

44 45 46

31

Station Lane

WARRINGTON
ROAD

22

A55
J32b
22
23

Halkyn/
Helygain

321

71

I

B5123

PO

2   Pant-y-gof

70

Travelodge

Plas
Newydd

3   Pen-y-
    parc

Bryn
garre

A55

Coed Lly

Bryn Eithin
Farm

B5123

4

69

Groes
Farm

Castell

5

Bryn-Y-Foel   PO

Enfys
Llys   Ffynnon
        Cae'r

Rhosesmor

Rhosesmor
Ind Est

B5123

6

Gwern-y-marl

368

321

Myna

22
23

Pen-yr-
Orsedd

Cefn-eurgain

I grid square represents 500 metres

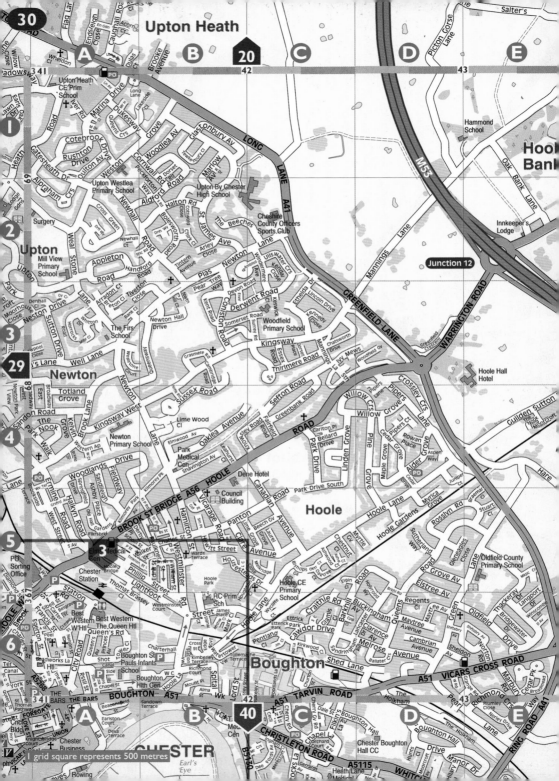

1 grid square represents 500 metres

Northop

F G H J K

23

24

2

3

4

5

34

6

Golf Course

Northop Golf & Country Club

Soughton Hall Hotel

Clawdd-Offa

Tyn-y-caeau

Soughton House

Soughton

NORTHOP ROAD

A5119

Ffordd Celyn

Vownog

Sychdyn Prim Sch

Wat's Dyke Way

Vownog Newydd

Pen-Y-Pentre

Longton Rd

Haulfryn

Ffordd Tirion

Maes Gwialig

Cae Glas

Ffordd Las

New Brighton Road

Pant Ucha

Pen-Y-Bryn

Black Brook

Manor Park

Tan-y-Coed

Bryn Teg

Ffordd Dawel

Tremy-y-Ffoel

Newbrighton Road

Chestnut Cl

Tyddynuchaf

The Laurels

Railkes Lane

A5119

MAIN ROAD

Llwyn Offa

Beaufort Park Hotel

New Brighton

A5119

Argoed View

Argoed Avenue

Gosmore Rd

Cae Isa

East Vw

Bryn Lane

Moor Cft

Moel Fammau Rd

Clwyd Crescent

Law Courts

County Hall

River Alyn

A5119

A494

Bryn-y-baal

Bryn-y-Baal Rd

Rockcliffe

Llys y Craig

Canol Y Bryn

Cherry Dr

Hill Vw

Bryn Rd

43

F G H J K

24 25 26

Maes-

J25 126

B5126

A55

B5126

J33a

67

68

66

365

F **G** **H** 27 **J** **K**

34 35 36

I

CHESTER ROAD

Beeches Farm

B5129

Cop House Farm

Rake Farm

2

Manor Crs

Brook Lane

Manor Lane

Manor Farm

Manor Farm

Llys Y Faenol

Cwrt Ogwen

3

Roodee

Hawarden Industrial Park

Castle Cl

Clwyd Cl

Hawarden Airport

38

Airfield Vw

Airfield View

Manor Lane Industrial Estate

Broughton Industrial Estate

Broughton Mills Road

4

Aircraft Factory

CHESTER ROAD

A5104

Hope's Place

Bretton Lane

5

ROAD

B5125

Lane

St Mary's Way

A5104

CHESTER ROAD

P

Cledwen Rd

Simonstone Rd

Broughton Shopping Park

3 64

Church Road

Bridge

A W

Simonstone Rd

Lane Dr

CHESTER ROAD

Eaton Close

Wynnstay Rd

Eaton

Broughton J&I School

Meadow Rd

Greenfield Rd

Clinic

Slatdeley

Hall

Somerford Rd

Broughton

A55

Deverdene Rd

Bretton Road

Bretton

6

MAIN ROAD

A5104

Main Road

Heron

Lynton

Gladstone

Pine Tree

Copper Beech

Congleton Road

Hawker

D C

Wellington Rd

Linden Avn

Road

Cil...

Bretton Dr

Y C

Matkney

Manor

Vale

35 36

F **G** **H** 47 **J** **K**

Broughton

A55

J35a

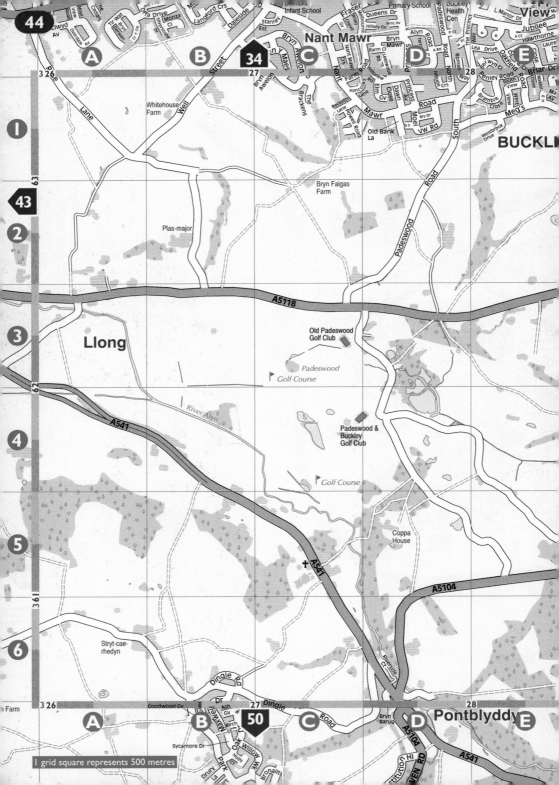

Broughton J&I School

A510

A55

Bretton Road

37

35

A55

J35a

36

I

2

Green End Farm

Brick Road

Lower Kinnerton

CH4

3

48

Bridge Farm

Moorend Farm

Moor Lane

4

Dodles Prin ol

5

PO

Croft Lane

6

New Hall Farm

Moor Lane

34

35

36

Cheshire County
Flintshire

Stringer's Lane

F **G** **H** **J** **K**

34

Broughton

F **G** **H** **J** **K**

48

A　B　38　C　D　E

336　37　38

I

63

Bretton Wood

2

A55

A5

CH4

Gorstella

Chester Southerly
Touring Park

Lache　Lane

LC

Roughlyn Crs

Roughill

3

Balderton

47

62

4

Greenwalls

Black
Wood

A483

Dodleston
CE Primary
School

5

St Mary's
Rd

Mallory Wk

Penfold Bordell

PO

Croft
Lane

361

Dodleston

Egerton
Wy

Croft

Church

Castle
Wy

Belgrave
Cl

Way

Belgrave

6

Moat
Farm

Pulford

A483

Belgrav

The Lache
Eyes

Decoy
Farm

Lache Lane

Park Lane

Bell Me
Busine

Cuckoo's
Nest

B5445

336　37　38

A　B　C　D　E

Oldfields
Farm

1 grid square represents 500 metres

Rowcliffe

Lache Hall Lnsdl
Crs

Merton Drive

Whaddon Dr

Greenacre Rd

The Kings School

F   **G**   **H**   **39**   **J**   **K**

39   40   41

Herons

Way

Kingsfield Ct

Chester Business Park

I

Eaton Road

Moat Farm

Herons

Council Building

Sandpiper Ct

2

Eccleston CE Primary School

Chester Approach

Hill Road

P+

Lakeside

Lakewood

Lakeside

Lakeside

Way

63

A483 WREXHAM ROAD

Rake Lane

3

62

Two Mile House

WREXHAM ROAD

The Rake

4

Chester Approach

B5445

Rake Lane

5

Belgrave Farm

ROAD

61

Garden Centre

Belgrave Avenue

Belgrave Avenue

Belgrave Avenue

6

F   **G**   **H**   **J**   **K**

39   40   41

Belgrave Mor Farm

Abbot's Meads....................29 H4
Allatni...............................34 B2
Aston................................25 K5
Backford...........................19 H2
Bagillt...............................9 H4
Balderton.........................48 D5
Belgrave...........................48 E6
Big Mancot.......................26 B6
Blacon..............................28 D2
Boughton..........................30 C6
Bretton.............................37 J6
Bridge Trafford..................21 J5
Broughton.........................47 G1
Brown Heath.....................41 K4
Bryn Celyn........................8 A1
Brymford..........................7 H6
Buckley.............................44 E1
Buckley Mountain...............34 D4
Burntwood Pentre...............35 F4
Bwlch................................10 C6
Calcoed............................7 G1
Carmel.............................7 G1
Cefn-Eurgain....................32 B1
Chester.............................3 H5
Christleton........................41 G2
Coed-Llai (Leeswood).........50 B2
Coed-Talon........................50 A4
Connah's Quay..................15 G6
Coppa View.......................34 E6
Dobs Hill...........................35 H6

Dodleston..........................48 A5
Dolphin.............................11 H1
Drury................................35 H5
Ewloe...............................35 H1
Ewloe Green......................25 F6
Flint Mountain...................23 G2
Flint (Y Fflint)...................13 J3
Gadlys..............................9 F6
Garden City.......................26 C1
Gian-y-Don.......................4 B1
Golch................................4 B6
Golftyn..............................15 F5
Gorsedd............................6 C1
Gorstella...........................48 A3
Greenfield (Maes-Glas).......5 F5
Guilden Sutton...................31 H3
Gwernymynydd...................42 B4
Halkyn Helygain.................12 A6
Handbridge........................40 A5
Hawarden..........................36 B2
Higher Kinnerton................46 C5
Higher Shotton...................25 H3
Holway.............................7 J1
Holywell (Treffynnon)..........8 B1
Hoole...............................30 C5
Hoole Bank........................30 E1
Hope(Yr Hûb).....................51 K5
Horeb...............................51 F6
Huntington.........................40 B4
Kelsterton.........................14 D5

Kinnerton Green.................46 E5
Lache...............................38 E5
Lane End...........................35 F6
Lea by Backford.................19 G2
Leadmill............................43 G2
Leeswood (Coed-Llai)..........50 B2
Licswm (Lixwm)..................10 A6
Little Heath........................41 G2
Little Mancot......................26 C6
Little Mountain...................45 H1
Littleton............................41 F1
Lixwm (Licswm)..................10 A6
Llannerch-y-mûr.................4 C2
Lloc.................................4 A4
Llong................................44 A3
Lower Kinnerton.................47 G3
Lower Mountain..................51 K3
Maes-Glas (Greenfield).......5 F5
Maes Pennant....................4 A2
Maes-y-Dre.......................43 F1
Mancot Royal.....................26 D5
Mickle Trafford..................21 G6
Milwr...............................8 B5
Mold................................42 D2
Mollington.........................18 D5
The Moor...........................36 C1
Moston.............................19 K5
Mount Pleasant..................13 F5
Mwdwl-Eithin....................7 G2
Mynydd Isa........................43 J1

Naid-y-March......................7 F4
Nant Mawr........................34 C6
New Brighton.....................33 K5
Newton.............................50 A3
Northop............................23 H6
Northop Hall......................24 D4
Oakenholt.........................14 A3
Old Warren........................36 C6
Pant................................6 B6
Pantasaph.........................6 D3
Pant y Wacco.....................6 B1
Pentre..............................26 C3
Pentre..............................43 H3
Pentre Bach.......................8 E2
Pentre Bagillt....................9 G4
Pentre Halkyn....................11 J3
Pen-Uchar Plwyf................10 D4
Pen-y-Ball Top...................7 H3
Penyffordd........................45 J5
Penymynydd......................45 K3
Picton..............................20 E3
Piper's Ash........................30 E4
Plemstall..........................21 K5
Pontblyddyn......................50 C1
Pontybodkin.......................50 B3
Prenbrigog........................34 A5
Pwll-Clai...........................11 F1
Pwll-Melyn........................10 F6
Queensferry......................26 B2
Queen's Park.....................3 J6

Rhosesmor.........................22
Rowton.............................41
Rowton Moor......................41
Saltney.............................38
Sandycroft........................26
Saughall...........................18
Sealand............................27
Shotton.............................25
Shotwick...........................16
Smithy Gate.......................7
Soughton..........................33
Spon Green........................45
Top Hill.............................7
Treffynnon (Holywell)...........7
Upton................................29
Upton Heath......................20
Vicarscross.......................31
Walwen............................10
Warren Mountain................44
Waverton...........................41
Wepre...............................25
Wervin..............................20
Whelston...........................11
Windmill...........................11
Y Fflint (Flint).....................13
Yr Hûb (Hope)....................51

USING THE STREET INDEX

Street names are listed alphabetically. Each street name is followed by its postal town or area locality, the Postcode District, the page number, and the reference to the square in which the name is found.

Standard index entries are shown as follows:

Abbey Gn *CH/BCN* CH1 ....2 D3

Street names and selected addresses not shown on the map due to scale restrictions are shown in the index with an asterisk:

Allerton Cl *CHSW/BR* CH4 * 45 K3

GENERAL ABBREVIATIONS

ACC	ACCESS	CTYD	COURTYARD	HLS	HILLS	MWY	MOTORWAY	SE	SOUTH E
ALY	ALLEY	CUTT	CUTTINGS	HO	HOUSE	N	NORTH	SER	SERVICE AF
AP	APPROACH	CV	COVE	HOL	HOLLOW	NE	NORTH EAST	SH	SHC
AR	ARCADE	CYN	CANYON	HOSP	HOSPITAL	NW	NORTH WEST	SHOP	SHOPP
ASS	ASSOCIATION	DEPT	DEPARTMENT	HRB	HARBOUR	O/P	OVERPASS	SKWY	SKYV
AV	AVENUE	DL	DALE	HTH	HEATH	OFF	OFFICE	SMT	SUMI
BCH	BEACH	DM	DAM	HTS	HEIGHTS	ORCH	ORCHARD	SOC	SOCI
BLDS	BUILDINGS	DR	DRIVE	HVN	HAVEN	OV	OVAL	SP	SP
BND	BEND	DRO	DROVE	HWY	HIGHWAY	PAL	PALACE	SPR	SPR
BNK	BANK	DRY	DRIVEWAY	IMP	IMPERIAL	PAS	PASSAGE	SQ	SQUA
BR	BRIDGE	DWGS	DWELLINGS	IN	INLET	PAV	PAVILION	ST	STR
BRK	BROOK	E	EAST	IND EST	INDUSTRIAL ESTATE	PDE	PARADE	STN	STAT
BTM	BOTTOM	EMB	EMBANKMENT	INF	INFIRMARY	PH	PUBLIC HOUSE	STR	STR
BUS	BUSINESS	EMBY	EMBASSY	INFO	INFORMATION	PK	PARK	STRD	STRA
BVD	BOULEVARD	ESP	ESPLANADE	INT	INTERCHANGE	PKWY	PARKWAY	SW	SOUTH W
BY	BYPASS	EST	ESTATE	IS	ISLAND	PL	PLACE	TDG	TRAD
CATH	CATHEDRAL	EX	EXCHANGE	JCT	JUNCTION	PLN	PLAIN	TER	TERR
CEM	CEMETERY	EXPY	EXPRESSWAY	JTY	JETTY	PLNS	PLAINS	THWY	THROUGH
CEN	CENTRE	EXT	EXTENSION	K	KING	PLZ	PLAZA	TNL	TUN
CFT	CROFT	F/O	FLYOVER	KNL	KNOLL	POL	POLICE STATION	TOLL	TOLL
CH	CHURCH	FC	FOOTBALL CLUB	L	LAKE	PR	PRINCE	TPK	TURNF
CHA	CHASE	FK	FORK	LA	LANE	PREC	PRECINCT	TR	TR
CHYD	CHURCHYARD	FLD	FIELD	LDG	LODGE	PREP	PREPARATORY	TRL	TR
CIR	CIRCLE	FLDS	FIELDS	LGT	LIGHT	PRIM	PRIMARY	TWR	TOV
CIRC	CIRCUS	FLS	FALLS	LK	LOCK	PROM	PROMENADE	U/P	UNDERP
CL	CLOSE	FM	FARM	LKS	LAKES	PRS	PRINCESS	UNI	UNIVER:
CLFS	CLIFFS	FT	FORT	LNDG	LANDING	PRT	PORT	UPR	UP
CMP	CAMP	FTS	FLATS	LT	LITTLE	PT	POINT		
CNR	CORNER	FWY	FREEWAY	LWR	LOWER	PTH	PATH	VA	VAL
CO	COUNTY	FY	FERRY	MAG	MAGISTRATE	PZ	PIAZZA	VIAD	VIADU
COLL	COLLEGE	GA	GATE	MAN	MANSIONS	QD	QUADRANT	VIS	VI
COM	COMMON	GAL	GALLERY	MD	MEAD	QU	QUEEN	VLG	VILL
COMM	COMMISSION	GDN	GARDEN	MDW	MEADOWS	QY	QUAY	VLLS	VILL
CON	CONVENT	GDNS	GARDENS	MEM	MEMORIAL	R	RIVER	VW	V
COT	COTTAGE	GLD	GLADE	MI	MILL	RBT	ROUNDABOUT	W	W
COTS	COTTAGES	GLN	GLEN	MKT	MARKET	RD	ROAD	WD	WC
CP	CAPE	GN	GREEN	MKTS	MARKETS	RDG	RIDGE	WHF	WHA
CPS	COPSE	GND	GROUND	ML	MALL	REP	REPUBLIC	WK	WA
CR	CREEK	GRA	GRANGE	MNR	MANOR	RES	RESERVOIR	WKS	WE
CREM	CREMATORIUM	GRG	GARAGE	MS	MEWS	RFC	RUGBY FOOTBALL CLUB	WLS	WE
CRS	CRESCENT	GT	GREAT	MSN	MISSION	RI	RISE	WY	W
CSWY	CAUSEWAY	GTWY	GATEWAY	MT	MOUNT	RP	RAMP	YD	YA
CT	COURT	GV	GROVE	MTN	MOUNTAIN	RW	ROW	YHA	YOUTH C
CTRL	CENTRAL	HGR	HIGHER	MTS	MOUNTAINS	S	SOUTH		
CTS	COURTS	HL	HILL	MUS	MUSEUM	SCH	SCHOOL		

POSTCODE TOWNS AND AREA ABBREVIATIONS

CH/BCN	Chester/Blacon	CHSW/BR	Chester southwest/	FLINT	Flint
CHNE	Chester northeast		Broughton	FROD/HEL	Frodsham/
CHSE	Chester southeast	CQ	Connah's Quay		Helsby

HLYW	Holywell	WRX/GR/LL	Wrexha
MOLD/BUCK	Mold/Buckley		Gresford/
NSTN	Neston	WRXW/BB	Wrexham west/Bryr

A

Abbey Gn *CH/BCN* CH1 ....2 D3
Abbey Sq *CH/BCN* CH1 ....2 D3
Abbey St *CH/BCN* CH1 ....2 E5
Abbots Cl *FLINT* CH6 ....9 H5
Abbot's Dr *CH/BCN* CH1 ....29 J4
Abbot's Gra *CHNE* CH2 ....29 J5
Abbots Knoll *CH/BCN* CH1 ....29 J4
Abbot's Nook *CHNE* CH2 ....7 D5
Abbots Pk *CH/BCN* CH1 ....29 J4
Abbots Wk *HLYW* CH8 ....8 B2
Abbotts Cl *CHSE* CH3 ....41 K5
Abbottsford Dr *CHSW/BR* CH4 ..45 H5

Abbotts La *CHSW/BR* CH4 ....45 H5
Abbotts Rd *CHSE* CH3 ....41 K5
Aber Crs *MOLD/BUCK* CH7 ....23 H6
Aberdaron Dr *CH/BCN* CH1 ....28 E5
Aber Las *FLINT* CH6 ....13 H5
Aberllanerch Dr
  MOLD/BUCK CH7 ....34 C4
Aber Rd *FLINT* CH6 ....13 F2
Aber Vw *CQ* CH5 ....14 E6
Abingdon Crs *CHSW/BR* CH4 ....39 F4
Acorn Ct *CHNE* CH2 ....29 J4
Acres La *CHNE* CH2 ....20 C6
Adder Hl *CHSE* CH3 ....40 D3
Adelaide Rd *CH/BCN* CH1 ....28 D4
Adwy Wynt *FLINT* CH6 ....13 H5
Ael y Bryn *MOLD/BUCK* CH7 ......42 E4

Afon Vw *CQ* CH5 ....14 E6
Agenora Cl *CQ* CH5 ....14 E6
Ainsdale Cl *MOLD/BUCK* CH7 ....34 C5
Airfield Vw *CQ* CH5 ....37 F4
Alamein Rd *CHNE* CH2 ....19 H5
Albert Av *FLINT* CH6 ....13 H4
Albert St *CH/BCN* CH1 ....3 G2
Albert St *MOLD/BUCK* CH7 ....50 A1
Albion Pl *CH/BCN* CH1 ....2 E6
Albion St *CH/BCN* CH1 ....2 E5
Alder Av *CQ* CH5 ....25 J5
Alderberry Rd *CQ* CH5 ....35 H3
Alder Gv *CHNE* CH2 ....30 D4
Alderley Pl *CH/BCN* CH1 ....28 E2
Aldersey Cl *CH/BCN* CH1 ....18 A5
Aldford Rd *CHNE* CH2 ....30 B2

Aled Crs *FLINT* CH6 ....13 F5
Aled Wy *CHSW/BR* CH4 ....38 D5
Alexandra Ct *MOLD/BUCK* CH7 ..34 E6
Alexandra Rd *MOLD/BUCK* CH7 ..43 F3
Alexandra St *CQ* CH5 ....25 K2
Allans Cl *CQ* CH5 ....26 A3
Allansford Av *CHSE* CH3 ....41 J6
Allerton Cl *CHSW/BR* CH4 * 45 K3
Allington La *CHSW/BR* CH4 ....40 A3
Allington Pl *CHSW/BR* CH4 ....40 A3
Alltami Rd *MOLD/BUCK* CH7 ......34 E5
Allt Goch *FLINT* CH6 ....13 G3
Allt-Goch La *FLINT* CH6 ....23 J1
Allt y Golch *HLYW* CH8 ....7 F1
Allt-y-Plas *HLYW* CH8 ....11 H4
Alma St *CHSE* CH3 ....3 K3

Almond Wy *WRX/GR/LL* LL12 5
Apraham Crs *CHNE* CH2 3
Alun Bank *MOLD/BUCK* CH7 4
Alun Cl *MOLD/BUCK* CH7 2
Alun Crs *CHSW/BR* CH4 3
Alvis Rd *CQ* CH5 2
Alwen Av *MOLD/BUCK* CH7 3
Alwen Dr *CQ* CH5 2
  FLINT CH6 ....
Alwyn Cl *MOLD/BUCK* CH7 4
Alwyn Gdns *CHNE* CH2 2
Alyn Bank *MOLD/BUCK* CH7 * 2
Alyndale *WRX/GR/LL* LL12 1
Alyndale Av *MOLD/BUCK* CH7 3
Alyndale Rd *CHSW/BR* CH4 4
Alyn Dr *CHSW/BR* CH4 ....

...rn Flds WRX/GR/LL LL12 ....51 H3
...rn Pk CQ CH5 ....35 H2
...rn Rd CHNE CH2 ....21 H5
MOLD/BUCK CH7 ....34 D6
...rn St MOLD/BUCK CH7 ....43 G2
...rn Vw MOLD/BUCK CH7 * 43 G2
...bleside CHNE CH4 ....30 B2
...bleside CI CQ CH5 ....24 E1
...brose Ter
MOLD/BUCK CH7 * 43 G3
...he Anchorage CHSE CH4 ....41 J5
...drew Crs CHSW/BR CH4 ....3 H7
...field CI CQ CH5 ....25 F4
...ne's Wy CHSW/BR CH4 ....3 K6
...wli CI CH/BCN CH1 ....18 A5
...pleby Dr CQ CH5 ....26 A6
...pleton Rd CHNE CH2 ....30 A2
...pleyards La CHSW/BR CH4 ....39 K5
...pleside CI CQ CH5 ....24 E1
...hur St CH/BCN CH1 ....29 C6
...n Bank CHNE CH4 ....30 E4
...nby PI CHNE CH4 ....30 A4
...Bellevue La CHNE CH4 ....31 F4
...nfield Crs CHSW/BR CH4 ....28 D3
CQ CH5 ....26 B6
...nfield Rd CQ CH5 ....25 K2
...n Gv CHSW/BR CH4 ....39 H5
CQ CH5 ....25 J3
FLINT CH6 ....13 J4
...ttern St MOLD/BUCK CH7 ....34 A5
...tt Rd CQ CH5 ....42 E2
...he Avenue CQ CH5 ....50 A1
...la CI CQ CH5 ....43 G3
...n Ct CQ CH5 ....25 F2
...n St CQ CH5 ....43 G4
...ondale Rd MOLD/BUCK CH7 ....43 G4
...onlea CI CHSW/BR CH4 ....38 E6
...el-y-Mor HLYW CH8 ....8 C2

B

...obage Rd CQ CH5 ....26 E4
...che Av CHNE CH2 ....29 J4
...he Dr CHNE CH2 ....29 K3
...hefield Av CHSE CH3 ....40 B4
...he Hall Ct CHNE CH2 ....40 C2
...chelor's La CHSW/BR CH4 ....39 C2
...k Queen St CH/BCN CH1 ....3 F5
...dgers CI CHSE CH3 ....41 G3
...dgers Ri CQ CH5 ....25 K2
...dgers Wk CHSW/BR CH4 ....20 A4
...ght Rd HLYW CH8 ....8 D1
...ley Bridge CI CHNE CH4 ....30 E4
...er Wy CHSE CH3 ....41 G3
...n Av HLYW CH8 ....5 H6
...later Crs CHSE CH3 ....30 D6
...lerat CI CH/BCN CH1 ....18 H3
...moral Cl FLINT CH6 ....12 E2
...moral Pk CH/BCN CH1 ....29 H4
...ton Av CQ CH5 ....30 A3
...La MOLD/BUCK CH7 ....35 H4
...nk Rd CQ CH5 ....15 F5
...nk Rw MOLD/BUCK CH7 ....35 F6
...nks Rd CHSW/BR CH4 ....36 B1
...k Vis MOLD/BUCK CH7 ....43 G4
...nnel La CHSW/BR CH4 ....43 J1
MOLD/BUCK CH7 ....45 G1
...ristow CI CHNE CH2 ....29 K5
...ley Cft CHSE CH3 ....30 C6
...mouth CI CQ CH5 ....24 E1
...nes CI CH/BCN CH1 ....20 C3
...nston Ct CHNE CH2 ....21 H6
...e Barnyard CQ CH5 ....25 K5
...tons CI CHSW/BR CH4 ....35 H5
...tons Ct CHSE CH3 ....29 J4
...ony Wy CHSW/BR CH4 ....38 E6
...tracks La CHSW/BR CH4 ....46 A3
...rrel Well HI CHSE CH3 ....3 K4
...he Bars CH/BCN CH1 ....3 G4
...tholomew Wy
CHSW/BR CH4 ....39 J4
...rcroft CI CQ CH5 ....26 D2
...twoods Dr CHSW/BR CH4 ....38 E5
...singwerk Av HLYW CH8 ....5 G4
...h St CH/BCN CH1 ....3 G4
...aconsfield Rd CQ CH5 ....25 J2
...aconsfield St CHSE CH3 ....3 H4
...aumaris Ld MOLD/BUCK CH7 ....34 E4
...aumaris Rd CQ CH5 ....24 E1

Beaumont Cl CHSW/BR CH4 ....38 E4
Beaver Cl CHSW/BR CH4 ....38 E5
Beckett's La CHSE CH3 ....40 C3
Becketts La MOLD/BUCK CH7 ....44 C1
Bedford Wy MOLD/BUCK CH7 ....42 E2
Bedward Rw CH/BCN CH1 ....3 F5
Beech Dr MOLD/BUCK CH7 ....42 E2
The Beeches CHNE CH4 * 30 B2
CH5 CH5 ....33 H2
CQ CH5 ....35 H3
HLYW CH8 ....5 H3
WRX/GR/LL LL12 ....51 J4
Beech Gv CHNE CH2 ....30 C5
FLINT CH6 ....13 J5
MOLD/BUCK CH7 ....34 A5
Beechlands Av CHSE CH4 ....40 C1
Beechley Rd CQ CH5 ....25 J5
Beech Rd CHSW/BR CH4 ....39 K5
Beechtree Rd MOLD/BUCK CH7 ....34 D5
Beechway CHNE CH4 ....29 J2
Beechwood Av CQ CH5 ....25 F1
Beechwood Cl
MOLD/BUCK CH7 ....42 E1
Beechwood Rd CHSW/BR CH4 ....38 D5
Beeston Pathway
CHNE CH4 ....40 A3
Beeston Rd CHSW/BR CH4 ....40 A3
Beeston Vw CHSW/BR CH4 ....40 A3
Belgrave Av CHSW/BR CH4 ....48 A6
Belgrave PI CHSW/BR CH4 ....49 F5
Belgrave Rd CHSE CH3 ....40 D2
Belgrave St CH/BCN CH1 ....29 C5
Bellard Dr CHNE 30 C4
Bellevue La CHNE CH4 ....31 F4
Belmont Av CQ CH5 ....25 H2
Belmont Crs MOLD/BUCK CH7 ....34 D4
Belmont Dr CHSW/BR CH4 ....38 B4
Belvedere CI CQ CH5 ....26 B3
Belvedere Dr CHSW/BR CH4 ....38 A4
Benllech CI CQ CH5 ....24 E1
Bennett's La CHSW/BR CH4 ....46 D5
CQ CH5 ....25 K6
Benton Dr CHNE CH2 ....7 J4
Berkley Dr CHSW/BR CH4 ....39 K4
Bernsdale Cl CQ CH5 ....26 D5
Berwyn Av CHSW/BR CH4 ....45 J6
Berwyn CI MOLD/BUCK CH7 ....34 A4
MOLD/BUCK CH7 ....58 E4
Bewley Ct CHSE CH3 ....40 C5
Bidston CI CHNE CH2 ....29 K3
Bilberry CI MOLD/BUCK CH7 ....34 B5
Birch CI MOLD/BUCK CH7 ....50 A1
Birch Ct MOLD/BUCK CH7 ....26 C6
The Birches CHSW/BR CH4 ....47 F1
Birchfield Crs CQ CH5 ....25 J3
Birch Heath La CHSE CH3 ....41 G2
Birch Rdg FLINT CH6 ....12 E4
Birch Ri CHNE CH2 ....29 K2
CQ CH5 ....35 K1
Birch Rd CHSW/BR CH4 ....47 F1
Birkdale Av MOLD/BUCK CH7 ....34 C4
Bishops CI CHNE CH2 ....37 G6
Bishop St CHNE CH2 ....30 B5
Bistre Av MOLD/BUCK CH7 ....34 D6
Bistre CI MOLD/BUCK CH7 ....34 D6
Black Brook Av CQ CH5 ....26 A6
Black Diamond St CH/BCN CH1 ....3 F1
Black Friars CH/BCN CH1 ....2 C6
Blackthorn CI CHSE CH3 ....40 C5
CHNE CH2 ....29 F1
Blacon Av CH/BCN CH1 ....27 F1
Blacon Hall Rd CH/BCN CH1 ....28 D5
Blacon Point Rd CH/BCN CH1 ....28 D5
Blaen Wern MOLD/BUCK CH7 ....42 B5
Blake CI CH/BCN CH1 ....29 F2
Blantern Rd CHSW/BR CH4 ....46 E5
Blenheim Ct CQ CH5 ....25 J2
Blossom Wy CHSW/BR CH4 ....38 D5
Bluebell CI CHSE CH3 ....40 D4
Bodlondeb FLINT CH6 ....13 H5
Bodnant Gv CHNE CH2 ....7 J4
Bold Pl CH/BCN CH1 ....3 F3
Bold Sq CH/BCN CH1 ....3 G3
Bolesworth Rd CHNE CH4 ....39 K5
Boleyn CI CH/BCN CH1 ....28 E2
Boilam CI CQ CH5 ....14 E6
Border Wy CHSE CH3 ....40 E1
Borough Gv FLINT CH6 ....13 H3
Bottoms La CHNE CH4 ....3 H7
Boughton CHNE CH2 ....3 J5
Boughton Hall Av CHSE CH3 ....40 C1
Boughton Hall Dr CHSE CH3 ....40 D1
The Boulevard CHSW/BR CH4 ....38 D5
Boundary La CHSW/BR CH4 ....38 D5
Bouverie St CH/BCN CH1 ....2 C3
Boxmoor CI CHSW/BR CH4 ....39 G5
Boydell Wy CHSW/BR CH4 ....48 A5
Bracken CI CHSW/BR CH4 ....47 G1
Brackendale Rd CQ CH5 ....26 B5
The Brackens CHSW/BR CH4 ....46 E4
MOLD/BUCK CH7 ....44 C1
Bradford St CHSW/BR CH4 ....39 K3
Bradshaw Av CHSE CH3 ....38 B3
Braemar CI CHSE CH3 ....30 E5
Braeside Av CQ CH5 ....26 A6
Bramble CI CHSE CH3 ....40 C3
MOLD/BUCK CH7 ....44 C1
The Brambles CQ CH5 ....25 K2
Bramley La CHSW/BR CH4 ....46 D5
Bramley Wy CQ CH5 ....35 H2
Brassey St CHSE CH3 ....3 K4
Bray Rd CQ CH5 ....25 H1
Breeze HI CQ CH5 ....25 H1
Brennus PI CH/BCN CH1 ....29 G6
Brentwood Rd CH/BCN CH1 ....28 E3
Breton CI CHNE 30 A3
Bretton Dr CHNE CH2 ....40 A3
Bretton La CHSW/BR CH4 ....37 J6
Bretton Rd CHSW/BR CH4 ....37 J6
Briar Dr MOLD/BUCK CH7 ....44 C1
Brickbarn CI MOLD/BUCK CH7 ....34 D5
Brickfield La CHSE CH3 ....31 H6
Brickfields MOLD/BUCK CH7 ....35 F6
Brick Rd CHSW/BR CH4 ....47 H2

Bridge Dr CHSE CH3 ....41 F3
Bridgeman Rd CH/BCN CH1 ....28 E5
Bridge PI CH/BCN CH1 ....2 E6
Bridge St CH/BCN CH1 ....2 E5
CHNE CH4 ....38 D5
CQ CH5 ....25 J1
MOLD/BUCK CH7 ....43 G2
Bridge Street Rw East
CH/BCN CH1 ....2 E5
Bridge Street Rw West
CH/BCN CH1 ....2 E5
Bridge Vw CQ CH5 ....26 D1
Bridgewater Dr CHSE CH3 ....30 E6
Brisbane Rd CH/BCN CH1 ....28 C4
Bristol CI CH/BCN CH1 ....28 C4
Britannia Rd MOLD/BUCK CH7 ....50 B2
Broadacre CI CHSE CH3 ....30 E6
Broad Oak Av CHSW/BR CH4 ....46 E1
Broad Oak CI CQ CH5 ....25 F2
Broadway CQ CH5 ....35 G4
Broadway East CHNE CH2 ....30 A3
Broadway West CHNE CH2 ....29 K3
Bro Alun MOLD/BUCK CH7 ....43 F2
Bro Deg FLINT CH6 ....13 F4
Brodie CI CHNE CH2 ....19 J5
Bro Dirion HLYW CH8 ....8 A2
Bromfield CI MOLD/BUCK CH7 ....43 G4
Bromfield La MOLD/BUCK CH7 ....43 G4
Bromfield Pk MOLD/BUCK CH7 ....43 G4
Bronalit MOLD/BUCK CH7 ....50 B1
Broncoed La MOLD/BUCK CH7 ....43 G5
Broncoed Pk MOLD/BUCK CH7 ....43 G5
Broncoed Ter
MOLD/BUCK CH7 * 43 G5
Bron Haul FLINT CH6 ....8 E2
Bron Llwyn FLINT CH6 ....13 G5
Bronte Gv CQ CH5 ....35 G2
Bron y Nant MOLD/BUCK CH7 ....43 G3
Bron-yr-Eglwys
MOLD/BUCK CH7 ....43 J3
Brony-Wern FLINT CH6 ....8 E2
Brookdale La CQ CH5 ....25 G2
FLINT CH6 ....13 F4
Brookdale Wy CHSE CH3 ....41 K5
Brooke Av MOLD/BUCK CH7 ....20 B6
Brooke CI CQ CH5 ....35 G2
Brookes Av CHSW/BR CH4 ....47 F1
Brookfield Dr MOLD/BUCK CH7 ....30 A4
Brookhill Wy MOLD/BUCK CH7 ....34 D5
Brook La CHNE CH2 ....29 J2
CQ CH5 ....37 G2
Brookleigh Av CQ CH5 ....26 B6
Brookmoore Ct CHNE CH2 ....29 J5
Brook Pl CH/BCN CH1 ....3 F2
Brook Rd CQ CH5 ....25 J2
Brookside CHSE CH3 ....40 C2
CQ CH5 ....24 B4
MOLD/BUCK CH7 ....35 F6
Brookside Ter CHNE CH2 ....29 K4
Brook St CH/BCN CH1 ....3 F2
Brook Street Br CHNE CH4 ....30 E5
Brook Street (Stroud-y-Nant)
MOLD/BUCK CH7 ....43 F3
Broughton Hall Rd
CHSW/BR CH4 ....47 G1
Broughton Mills Rd
CHSW/BR CH4 ....37 K4
Browning CI CH/BCN CH1 ....29 F2
Brown's La CHSW/BR CH4 ....39 J3
Brunswick Rd MOLD/BUCK CH7 ....34 D5
Brunswood Gv FLINT CH6 ....12 E4
Brushwood Av CHSW/BR CH4 ....43 K2
Bryn Aber FLINT CH6 ....9 H5
HLYW CH8 ....7 K2
Bryn Aelwyd Ucha HLYW CH8 ....7 G1
Bryn Afon HLYW CH8 ....5 F6
Bryn Aur HLYW CH8 ....6 C5
Bryn Awel HLYW CH8 ....11 H4
Bryn Awelon MOLD/BUCK CH7 ....43 G3
Bryn Barug MOLD/BUCK CH7 ....50 C1
Bryn Cae PI CQ CH5 * 15 G6
Bryn Cerrig HLYW CH8 ....11 H4
Bryn Clwyd MOLD/BUCK CH7 ....43 K1
Bryn Clyd MOLD/BUCK CH7 ....50 A2
Bryn Coch Crs MOLD/BUCK CH7 ....42 E4
Bryn Coch La MOLD/BUCK CH7 ....42 E4
Bryn Coch Uchaf Upper
Bryn Coch) MOLD/BUCK CH7 ....42 D4
Bryn-Coed-Wepre CQ CH5 ....14 E6
Canol y Bryn MOLD/BUCK CH7 ....34 A3
Bryn Derw FLINT CH6 ....13 H5
Bryn Derwen MOLD/BUCK CH7 ....34 A6
Bryn Dr CQ CH5 ....26 A6
Bryn Dyffryn HLYW CH8 ....7 J2
Bryn Dyrys FLINT CH6 ....9 H5
Bryn Eglwys FLINT CH6 ....23 G2
Bryn Eithin CQ CH5 ....16 B6
HLYW CH8 ....11 H4
Bryn Felin HLYW CH8 ....11 H3
Brynford HI HLYW CH8 ....7 G5
Brynford Rd HLYW CH8 ....11 C3
Brynford St HLYW CH8 ....8 A3
Bryn Garmon MOLD/BUCK CH7 ....43 K1
Bryn Glas FLINT CH6 ....12 E5
Bryn Gwyn FLINT CH6 ....9 H4
Bryn-Gwyn La
MOLD/BUCK CH7 ....24 C3
Bryn Helig FLINT CH6 ....13 H5
Bryn Heulog MOLD/BUCK CH7 ....42 E5
Bryn Hilyn La MOLD/BUCK CH7 ....43 K1
Bryn Hyfryd CQ CH5 ....24 E2
MOLD/BUCK CH7 ....43 G4
Bryn La MOLD/BUCK CH7 ....33 J6
Bryn Mawr CHSW/BR CH4 ....34 D6
Bryn Mawr Rd HLYW CH8 ....11 J3
Bryn Mor Dr FLINT CH6 ....13 F4
Bryn Noddfa MOLD/BUCK CH7 ....43 J3
Bryn Offa MOLD/BUCK CH7 ....43 K1
Bryn Onnen FLINT CH6 ....9 H5
Bryn Rhyd MOLD/BUCK CH7 ....23 G6
Bryn Rd CQ CH5 ....14 E6
FLINT CH6 ....13 C4
Bryn Seion La MOLD/BUCK CH7 ....33 G4
Bryn Siriol FLINT CH6 ....13 H4

C

Cable St CQ CH5 ....15 G6
Cadnant CI CQ CH5 ....14 F4
Cadnant Ct (Llys Cadnant)
CHSW/BR CH4 ....37 H5
Cadnant Dr FLINT CH6 ....9 F4
Cae Berwyn MOLD/BUCK CH7 ....33 H4
Cae Bracty MOLD/BUCK CH7 ....43 F3
Cae Bychan FLINT CH6 ....13 J5
Cae Derw FLINT CH6 ....13 H4
Cae Eithin HLYW CH8 ....10 B5
Cae Fawnog CHSW/BR CH4 ....30 D5
Cae Glas MOLD/BUCK CH7 ....42 D4
Cae Gwynedd HLYW CH8 ....5 F6
Cae Haf MOLD/BUCK CH7 ....24 C4
Cae Helyg HLYW CH8 ....11 H3
Cae Hir FLINT CH6 ....13 J5
Cae Isa MOLD/BUCK CH7 ....33 J6
Cae Llys CI CQ CH5 ....24 E3
Cae Masarn HLYW CH8 ....11 H4
Cae-Mefus HLYW CH8 ....7 K3
Cae'r Ffynnon FLINT CH6 ....8 E2
Caernarvon CI CQ CH5 ....25 K3
Cae'r Onnen HLYW CH8 ....11 H3
Caergilly Rd MOLD/BUCK CH7 ....34 C6
Cae'r Rhos MOLD/BUCK CH7 ....22 A6
Caesar Av FLINT CH6 ....13 J4
Cae-y-Dderwen HLYW CH8 ....8 A1
Cairndale Av CQ CH5 ....25 F1
Cairns Crs CH/BCN CH1 ....29 F2
Cairnton Crs HLYW CH8 ....5 H6
Caldbeck Crs CQ CH5 ....24 E1
Caldias CI CQ CH5 ....24 E4
Caldy Av CQ CH5 ....24 E2
Caldy CI CHNE CH2 ....29 K2
Caldy Valley Rd CHSE CH3 ....40 D4
Cambrian Av CHSW/BR CH4 ....30 D6
Cambrian CI CQ CH5 ....25 G1
MOLD/BUCK CH7 ....50 A1
Cambrian Rd CH/BCN CH1 ....2 B2
Cambridge Wy CQ CH5 ....24 E3
Cambridge Rd CHNE CH2 ....30 B3
Campion CI CHSE CH3 ....40 D4
Camrose CI CQ CH5 ....24 E3
Canadian Av CHNE CH2 ....30 C4
Canal Side CH/BCN CH1 ....3 F3
Canal St CH/BCN CH1 ....2 C3
Canberra Wy CH/BCN CH1 ....28 D4
Canning St CH/BCN CH1 ....2 D3
Cannon Wy CHSW/BR CH4 ....46 D5
Canol y Bryn MOLD/BUCK CH7 ....34 A3
Canterbury Rd CH/BCN CH1 ....29 F3
Capeland CI CHSW/BR CH4 ....38 D5
Capesthorne Rd CHSE CH3 ....41 K5
Carlines Av CQ CH5 ....24 E2
Carlisle Rd CH/BCN CH1 ....28 E3
Carlton Av CHSW/BR CH4 ....38 D4
Carlton CI CHNE CH2 ....21 G6
Carlton PI CHNE CH2 ....30 A4
Carmel CI CH/BCN CH1 ....28 D5
Carmel Rd HLYW CH8 ....11 H4
Carrick Rd CHSW/BR CH4 ....39 G5
Carter St CH/BCN CH1 ....3 H3
Carton Rd MOLD/BUCK CH7 ....43 K3
Castle CI CQ CH5 ....25 H5
Castle Croft Rd CHSW/BR CH4 ....39 H5
Castle Dyke St FLINT CH6 ....13 H2
Castle Flds CQ CH5 ....25 H5
Castle La CHSW/BR CH4 ....25 K4
Castle Park Av CQ CH5 ....25 H5
Castle PI CH/BCN CH1 ....2 E6
Castle Ri CQ CH5 ....36 B2
Castle St CH/BCN CH1 ....2 D6
FLINT CH6 ....13 H3
Castle Wy CHSW/BR CH4 ....48 A6
Catherine Dr CQ CH5 ....24 E3
Catherine St CH/BCN CH1 ....2 B1
Cavalier Dr CH/BCN CH1 ....28 D4
Cavalier Dr FLINT CH6 ....13 H4
Cavendish Ct CHSW/BR CH4 ....39 C5
Cavendish Rd CHSW/BR CH4 ....39 C5
Cawdor Dr CHSW/BR CH4 ....30 C6
Cecil St CHSE CH3 ....40 C1

Bryn Teg HLYW CH8 ....8 C2
MOLD/BUCK CH7 ....33 G4
Bryn Tirion HLYW CH8 ....10 C6
Bryntirion Rd FLINT CH6 ....9 H6
Bryntirion Rd HLYW CH8 ....12 B1
Brynwood Dr MOLD/BUCK CH7 ....44 D1
Bryn-y-Baal Rd
MOLD/BUCK CH7 ....43 K1
Bryn-y-Coed HLYW CH8 ....8 A2
Bryn-y-Felin HLYW CH8 ....24 A5
Bryn-y-Foel MOLD/BUCK CH7 ....43 K1
Bryn-y-Gwynt HLYW CH8 ....11 J4
Buckingham Av CHSE CH3 ....30 C6
Bulkeley St CHSE CH3 ....40 C1
Bumper's La CH/BCN CH1 ....28 A4
Bunce St CH/BCN CH1 ....2 D6
Burgess Dr CH/BCN CH1 ....28 A4
Burges St CHNE CH2 ....30 B5
Burnham Rd CHSW/BR CH4 ....39 F4
Burns CI CQ CH5 ....35 G2
Burns Wy CH/BCN CH1 ....29 F2
Burntwood Ct
MOLD/BUCK CH7 ....35 G4
Burntwood Rd
MOLD/BUCK CH7 ....35 G4
Burton Dr CHSW/BR CH4 ....46 D5
Burton Rd CHSE CH3 ....41 G3
Butcher's La CHSE CH3 ....41 G3
Butler St CQ CH5 ....25 K3
Butterbache Rd CHSE CH3 ....40 C4
Butterbur CI CHSE CH3 ....40 C4
Buttermere CI CQ CH5 ....24 E1
Buxton La HLYW CH8 ....11 C5
Byron CI CH/BCN CH1 ....28 E2
CQ CH5 ....25 F3
Bythom CI CHSE CH3 ....41 G3

Cedar Av CQ CH5 ....14 E5
CQ CH5 ....26 E1
Cedar CI MOLD/BUCK CH7 ....34 D5
Cedar Dr CHNE CH2 ....30 D4
Cedar Gdns CQ CH5 ....25 J5
Cedar Gv CHNE CH2 ....30 D4
MOLD/BUCK CH7 ....42 E2
Cedar Ms CH/BCN CH1 ....28 E4
Cedar Pk CHSE CH3 ....30 E6
The Cedars (Y Cedrwydd)
MOLD/BUCK CH7 ....24 A6
Cefna CI CQ CH5 ....24 E3
Cefn La FLINT CH6 ....11 K1
HLYW CH8 ....8 A2
Cefn Rd CQ CH5 ....15 F6
CQ CH5 ....35 H1
Celandine CI CHSE CH3 ....40 C3
Celtic St CQ CH5 ....25 J1
Celyn Crs CHSW/BR CH4 ....38 D5
Celyn Dr WRX/GR/LL LL12 ....51 H6
Celyn La HLYW CH8 ....7 F1
Celyn Pk HLYW CH8 ....7 F1
Cement PI CH/BCN CH1 * 3 F5
Cemlyn CI CH/BCN CH1 ....28 E5
Central Dr CQ CH5 ....25 K3
Cestrian St CQ CH5 ....15 H6
Chain Maker's Rw
CHSW/BR CH4 ....38 E3
Challinor St CHSE CH3 ....40 C1
Chambers La MOLD/BUCK CH7 ....43 K2
Chancel Dr FLINT CH6 ....9 H6
Chandos CI CHSW/BR CH4 ....40 A4
Chapel CI CH/BCN CH1 ....18 A5
CHSE CH3 ....41 J3
Chapel La CHSE CH3 ....40 C1
Chapel St CHSE CH3 ....3 H3
CQ CH5 ....25 C1
CQ CH5 ....25 G6
Chapel St (Stryd-y-Capel)
MOLD/BUCK CH7 ....43 F3
Charles Crs CHSW/BR CH4 ....3 H7
Charles Dr FLINT CH6 ....13 H4
Charles Rd CHNE CH7 ....19 H6
MOLD/BUCK CH7 ....50 B2
Charles St CH/BCN CH1 ....3 F5
CHNE CH2 ....3 J1
MOLD/BUCK CH7 ....43 F5
Charlotte St CH/BCN CH1 ....2 B3
Charterhall Dr CHNE CH2 ....8 J3
Chaser Ct CH/BCN CH1 ....29 F5
The Chase CHSW/BR CH4 ....36 D5
Chaucer CI CH/BCN CH1 ....28 E2
Chelford CI CH/BCN CH1 ....29 F5
Chemistry La CQ CH5 ....26 C4
Cheriton CI CQ CH5 ....24 E4
Cherry Dale Rd CHSW/BR CH4 ....46 E1
Cherry Gv MOLD/BUCK CH7 ....43 K1
Cherry Grove Rd CHSE CH3 ....40 C1
Cherry Orchard Rd
CHNE CH4 ....36 B5
Cherry Rd CHSE CH3 ....40 C1
Chesham St CH/BCN CH1 * 3 G2
Cheshire La MOLD/BUCK CH7 ....34 D4
Cheshire Vw CHSW/BR CH4 ....40 A5
Chester Ap CHSW/BR CH4 ....49 K5
Chester CI CQ CH5 ....25 K3
Chester Rd CHNE CH2 ....30 D4
CHSE CH4 ....45 J4
CQ CH5 ....26 D5
CQ CH5 ....35 K6
FLINT CH6 ....13 H5
MOLD/BUCK CH7 ....43 G3
Chester Road(East) CQ CH5 ....26 B3
Chester Road (West) CQ CH5 ....25 K2
Chester St CHSW/BR CH4 ....3 G2
FLINT CH6 ....13 H3
MOLD/BUCK CH7 ....43 F3
Chester St (Heol Caer)
FLINT CH6 ....13 G3
Chesterton Av CQ CH5 ....35 G2
Chesterton Ct CHNE CH2 ....29 K4
Chestnut CI CHNE CH2 ....30 C5
FLINT CH6 ....13 H4
MOLD/BUCK CH7 ....33 F5
Chestnut Crs CQ CH5 ....35 G5
Chestnut Gv CQ CH5 ....26 A6
Chestnut Rd MOLD/BUCK CH7 ....42 D4
Chevron Hey CH/BCN CH1 ....28 D4
Chevrons Wy CQ CH5 ....25 K3
Cheyney Rd CH/BCN CH1 ....2 B1
Chichester St CH/BCN CH1 ....2 E1
Chiltern CI CHSW/BR CH4 ....39 H5
CQ CH5 ....25 G1
Chirk CI CHNE CH2 ....30 B2
Christleton Rd CHSE CH3 ....40 C1
Church CI MOLD/BUCK CH7 ....24 B4
MOLD/BUCK CH7 ....34 B4
Church Croft CHSW/BR CH4 ....48 A6
Church College CI CH/BCN CH1 ....29 H5
Church Ct CHSW/BR CH4 ....39 J5
Church Hall CI CH/BCN CH1 ....29 F4
Church La CHNE CH2 ....15 G6
CQ CH5 ....35 J2
Church Ms CHSW/BR CH4 ....36 B2
Church Rd CH/BCN CH1 ....18 A5
CHSW/BR CH4 ....37 G6
CQ CH5 ....26 C5
MOLD/BUCK CH7 ....34 E4
Church St CH/BCN CH1 ....3 F1
CQ CH5 ....14 E5
FLINT CH6 ....13 G3
Church Vw CQ CH5 ....26 C5
Church Wk FLINT CH6 ....9 H5
Church Wks CHSE CH3 ....41 G2
Churchward CI CHNE CH2 ....29 K4
Cil Coed CHSE CH3 ....28 E3
Cilcain Rd MOLD/BUCK CH7 ....42 D5
Cinder CI CHSE CH3 ....31 H3
Cinder La CHSE CH3 ....31 H4
Circular Dr CHSW/BR CH4 ....58 E6
CQ CH5 ....25 G6

City Rd CH/BCN CH1 .... 3 C3
City Walls CH/BCN CH1 .... 2 E3
City Walls Rd CH/BCN CH1 .... 2 C4
Clair Av CO CH5 .... 26 E5
Clare Av CHSE CH3 .... 30 B5
Claremont Av CO CH5 .... 26 C5
Clarence Av CHSE CH3 .... 30 C6
Clarence St CO CH5 .... 25 K3
Clarendon Cl CHSW/BR CH4 .... 40 A4
Clay Hill La CO CH5 .... 26 A4
Clayhall Av MOLD/BUCK CH7 .... 39 H5
Claypits La CHSE CH3 .... 41 H6
Clayton Cl CHSW/BR CH4 .... 42 E5
Clayton Rd MOLD/BUCK CH7 .... 42 E3
Cleaver Rd CO CH5 .... 26 D2
Cledwen Av MOLD/BUCK CH7 .... 34 A5
Cledwen Rd CHSW/BR CH4 .... 37 G5
Cleveland Gv CO CH5 .... 26 C2
Cleves Cl CH/BCN CH1 .... 28 D2
Clifford Dr CHSW/BR CH4 .... 40 D5
Clifton Dr CH/BCN CH1 .... 28 E5
Cliveden Rd CHSW/BR CH4 .... 39 F5
Clivedon Rd CO CH5 .... 24 E2
Clos Coed CO CH5 .... 26 A6
The Close HLYW CH8 .... 18 A5
  CO CH5 .... 35 J1
  HLYW CH8 .... 5 G5
Clos y Fferm FLINT CH6 .... 42 E4
Clos y Meillion CO CH5 .... 35 H2
Clover La CHSW/BR CH4 .... 39 F5
Clover Pl CHSW/BR CH4 .... 39 F5
Clwyd Av HLYW CH8 .... 9 F6
  MOLD/BUCK CH7 .... 34 A6
Clwyd Cl CHSE CH3 .... 37 F4
Clwyd Crs MOLD/BUCK CH7 .... 33 J6
Clwyd Gv MOLD/BUCK CH7 .... 34 C6
Clydyd St CO CH5 .... 25 K4
Clydesdale Rd
  MOLD/BUCK CH7 .... 35 H5
Coalpit La CHSW/BR CH4 .... 18 C3
Coatings By-Pass Rd CO CH5 .... 15 H6
Coatings Two CO CH5 .... 15 H5
The Cobbles CHSW/BR CH4 .... 39 K3
Coed Bach FLINT CH6 .... 13 F4
Coed Onn Rd FLINT CH6 .... 13 G4
Coed Terfin MOLD/BUCK CH7 .... 45 J2
Coed-y-Fron HLYW CH8 .... 7 J3
Coed y Graig CHSW/BR CH4 .... 45 J2
Colchester Sq CHSW/BR CH4 .... 39 F5
Colehill Pl CO CH5 .... 15 J6
Coleridge Cl CHSE CH3 .... 29 G5
Coleshill La FLINT CH6 .... 9 J6
Coleshill St FLINT CH6 .... 13 G2
  HLYW CH8 .... 8 A5
Colinwood Av CHSW/BR CH4 .... 40 C4
College Gn CHSW/BR CH4 .... 39 K3
College Vw CO CH5 .... 14 E5
Colliers La MOLD/BUCK CH7 .... 34 A5
Colliery La CO CH5 .... 24 E6
Colson Ct CHNE CH2 .... 2 D1
Coltsfoot Cl CHSE CH3 .... 40 C5
Columbine Cl CHSE CH3 .... 40 C4
Commonhall St CH/BCN CH1 .... 2 D5
Common La CHSE CH3 .... 41 J6
Compton Pl CHSW/BR CH4 .... 39 G4
Congleton Rd CHSW/BR CH4 .... 37 G6
Coniston Cl CO CH5 .... 24 E2
Coniston Rd CHNE CH2 .... 30 B3
Connahs Quay Rd
  MOLD/BUCK CH7 .... 25 J6
Connaught Av CO CH5 .... 25 K2
Coniston Dr MOLD/BUCK CH7 .... 34 E5
Constitution Hl
  MOLD/BUCK CH7 .... 50 C1
Conway Av MOLD/BUCK CH7 .... 45 F1
Conway Cl CHSW/BR CH4 .... 38 D5
  FLINT CH6 .... 13 G2
Conway Ct CO CH5 .... 24 E1
Conway St MOLD/BUCK CH7 .... 40 C3
Coopers Cft CHSE CH3 .... 40 C3
Cooper's La CO CH5 .... 15 F5
Copeswood Cl CHSW/BR CH4 .... 40 C3
Coppack Cl CO CH5 .... 24 E3
Coppafield Cl MOLD/BUCK CH7 .... 35 F6
Coppa Vw MOLD/BUCK CH7 .... 34 E6
Copper Beach Cl
  CHSW/BR CH4 .... 47 G1
The Coppice CO CH5 .... 25 H6
Coppins Cl CHSE CH3 .... 30 C6
The Copse CO CH5 .... 35 H2
Cornist Dr FLINT CH6 .... 13 F3
Cornist La FLINT CH6 .... 13 F3
Cornist Rd FLINT CH6 .... 13 F3
Cornwall Rd CHNE CH2 .... 30 A1
  CO CH5 .... 25 K4
Cornwall St CH/BCN CH1 .... 2 C2
Coronation Av CHSW/BR CH4 .... 47 F1
Coronation St FLINT CH6 .... 13 G2
Corporation St FLINT CH6 .... 13 G2
Corun y Bryn CO CH5 .... 24 E3
Corwen Cl CO CH5 .... 24 E2
Corwen Rd CHSW/BR CH4 .... 45 H5
  MOLD/BUCK CH7 .... 50 B3
Corwen Wy CHSW/BR CH4 .... 45 J5
Cotebrook Dr CHNE CH2 .... 30 A1
Cotes Pl CH/BCN CH1 .... 28 E5
Cotgreaves Cl CHSW/BR CH4 .... 39 H5
Cotswold Cl CHNE CH2 .... 30 B2
Cottage Gdns MOLD/BUCK CH7 .... 35 F6
Cottage La CO CH5 .... 26 C6
Cottage Rd CHSW/BR CH4 .... 39 H5
Cotterill Cl CO CH5 .... 25 F3
Countess Wy CH/BCN CH1 .... 29 J4
County Rd MOLD/BUCK CH7 .... 50 B2
Courtet Dr CO CH5 .... 26 C6
Courtland Dr CO CH5 .... 25 J5
Courtney Rd CHSW/BR CH4 .... 38 E6
Cousens Wy CHSW/BR CH4 .... 29 H4
Cowhey Cl CHSW/BR CH4 .... 39 H5
Cowthorne Dr CHSE CH3 .... 41 J5
Crabwall Pl CHNE CH2 .... 29 F5
Craithie Rd CHNE CH2 .... 30 C6
Cranbrook Cl CO CH5 .... 25 G2
Cranbrook Cl CO CH5 .... 25 G2
Cranleigh Crs CHNE CH2 .... 29 H4
Crawford's Wk CHNE CH2 .... 3 J1
Crecas La HLYW CH8 .... 7 G1
The Crescent CHNE CH2 .... 29 K4
Crewe St CH/BCN CH1 .... 3 G2

Cricceth Cl MOLD/BUCK CH7 .... 34 E3
Croes Atti La FLINT CH6 .... 13 J4
Croft Av CO CH5 .... 25 G2
Croft Cl CHSE CH3 .... 41 J5
Crofters Pk CO CH5 .... 26 C6
Crofters Wy CH/BCN CH1 .... 17 K6
  CO CH5 .... 26 C6
Croft La CHSW/BR CH4 .... 47 K5
The Croft CHNE CH2 .... 29 K3
Crompton Cl CHSW/BR CH4 .... 46 D5
Cromwell Av MOLD/BUCK CH7 .... 34 C4
Cromwell Cl CHSW/BR CH4 .... 45 J4
  CO CH5 .... 25 J4
Crookenden Cl CHNE CH2 .... 19 J5
Crookenden Rd CHNE CH2 .... 19 J5
Crook St CH/BCN CH1 .... 2 D4
Crosfield HLYW CH8 .... 5 F6
Cross Gn CHNE CH2 .... 30 A2
Cross Hey CHSW/BR CH4 .... 38 H7
Crossley Crs CHSE CH3 .... 30 D5
Cross Roads HLYW CH8 .... 8 A3
Cross St CHNE CH2 .... 3 J2
Cross Tree Cl CO CH5 .... 36 B2
Cross Tree Ct MOLD/BUCK CH7 .... 37 F3
Crosstree La CO CH5 .... 36 B1
Crossway CO CH5 .... 25 H6
Crossways CHSW/BR CH4 .... 45 J5
Crud-y-Cwynt MOLD/BUCK CH7 .... 34 A6
Cunliffe St MOLD/BUCK CH7 .... 45 F4
Cuppin St CH/BCN CH1 .... 2 D5
Curzon Cl CHSW/BR CH4 .... 39 G2
Curzon Pk North CHSW/BR CH4 ...... 2 A7
Curzon Pk South
  CHSW/BR CH4 .... 39 G3
Curzon St CHSW/BR CH4 .... 39 F3
Cwm Cl MOLD/BUCK CH7 .... 45 J1
Cwm Eithion FLINT CH6 .... 13 H5
Cwrt Brenig MOLD/BUCK CH7 .... 35 H1
Cwrt Cwellyn CO CH5 .... 37 F5
Cwrt Dewi Sant HLYW CH8 .... 6 F3
Cwrt Dinas CO CH5 .... 35 F3
Cwrt Leighton (Leighton Ct)
  CO CH5 .... 15 G6
Cwrt Ogwen CO CH5 .... 35 G1
Cwrt Onnen CO CH5 .... 26 C6
Cwrt Rhos-Lan CO CH5 .... 26 C6
Cwrt y Mynach
  MOLD/BUCK CH7 .... 43 F2
Cyman Cl CH/BCN CH1 .... 28 D5

D

Dafydd Cl MOLD/BUCK CH7 .... 34 A4
Daisy Hill Rd MOLD/BUCK CH7 .... 34 E6
Dale Dr CHNE CH2 .... 19 K6
Dale Rd CO CH5 .... 19 K6
Daleside CHNE CH2 .... 19 K6
  MOLD/BUCK CH7 .... 34 B6
Dale St CHSE CH3 .... 40 C1
Dalton Cl CH/BCN CH1 .... 28 E5
Dane Cl CHSW/BR CH4 .... 39 F5
Dane Gv CHNE CH2 .... 21 H6
Daniell Wy CHSE CH3 .... 40 C3
Daniel Owen Sq
  MOLD/BUCK CH7 * 43 F3
Darlington Cl CH/BCN CH1 .... 18 A5
Darwen Dr CHSW/BR CH4 .... 45 K3
Darwin Rd CH/BCN CH1 .... 28 A6
Daulwyn Rd MOLD/BUCK CH7 .... 35 G4
Dauncey Cl CHNE CH2 .... 19 J5
Dawn Cl MOLD/BUCK CH7 .... 44 D1
Dawpool Cl CHNE CH2 .... 29 J5
Dawson Dr CHNE CH2 .... 29 J5
Daytona Dr MOLD/BUCK CH7 .... 24 C4
Ddol Awel MOLD/BUCK CH7 .... 42 D3
Ddreiniog Rd HLYW CH8 .... 7 F1
Deanery Cl CHSW/BR CH4 .... 39 K3
Deans Av CO CH5 .... 15 H5
Deansbury Cl FLINT CH6 .... 13 E3
Deans Ct CHNE CH2 .... 29 K2
  FLINT CH6 .... 9 H6
Deans Pl CO CH5 .... 25 H1
Dee Av CHSW/BR CH4 .... 46 E4
Dee Banks CHSE CH3 .... 40 B3
Dee Fords Av CHSE CH3 .... 40 C1
Dee Hills Pk CHSE CH3 .... 3 H4
Dee Pk CHSE CH3 .... 3 H4
Dee Rd CHNE CH2 .... 21 H5
  CO CH5 .... 25 H2
  CO CH5 .... 26 D1
Deeside Crs CH/BCN CH1 .... 27 J3
Deeside La CH/BCN CH1 .... 27 J3
Dee Vw CO CH5 .... 26 A4
Dee View Rd CO CH5 .... 15 F5
Deganwy Cl MOLD/BUCK CH7 .... 34 E3
Degas Cl CO CH5 .... 14 E6
Deiniol's Rd CO CH5 .... 26 C6
Delamere Av MOLD/BUCK CH7 .... 45 F1
Delamere St CH/BCN CH1 .... 3 G2
The Dell CHSE CH3 .... 31 H3
Delta Cl CHSW/BR CH4 .... 38 E4
Delves Wk CHSE CH3 .... 40 D5
Delvine Dr CHNE CH2 .... 29 K2
Delyn Rd HLYW CH8 .... 5 F6
Demage La CHNE CH2 .... 19 F2
  CO CH5 .... 19 K6
Denbigh Cl MOLD/BUCK CH7 .... 34 E3
Denbigh Rd MOLD/BUCK CH7 .... 42 E1
Denbigh St CHSW/BR CH4 .... 2 B1
Denford St CHSW/BR CH4 .... 37 G6
Denhall Cl CHNE CH2 .... 29 J4
Dennis Dr CHSW/BR CH4 .... 39 H4
Denson Dr CO CH5 .... 25 J6
Denstone Dr CHSW/BR CH4 .... 39 G6
Dentith Dr CH/BCN CH1 .... 28 E5
Derby Pl CHNE CH2 .... 3 K2
Derby Rd WRX/GR/LL LL12 .... 51 H6
Derwen Cl CO CH5 .... 15 G6
Derwen Deg MOLD/BUCK CH7 .... 50 B2
Derwent Rd CO CH5 .... 30 B3
Deva Av CHSW/BR CH4 .... 38 E4
  CO CH5 .... 25 F1
  HLYW CH8 .... 8 A2
Deva Cl FLINT CH6 .... 13 J4
Deva La CHNE CH2 .... 29 J2
Deva Link CH/BCN CH1 .... 29 G6

Deva Ter CHSE CH3 .... 3 H4
Devon Pl CO CH5 .... 25 F2
Devon Rd CHNE CH2 .... 30 B3
Devonshire Pl CHSW/BR CH4 .... 39 K3
Devonshire Rd CHSW/BR CH4 .... 37 G6
Dewi Av HLYW CH8 .... 7 K3
Dicksons Dr CHNE CH2 .... 29 K3
Dig La CO CH5 .... 36 B2
Dinas Cl CH/BCN CH1 .... 28 D5
Dinghouse MOLD/BUCK CH7 .... 35 G3
Dinghouse Wd
  MOLD/BUCK CH7 .... 35 G4
Dingle Bank CHSW/BR CH4 .... 39 J3
Dingle Rd MOLD/BUCK CH7 .... 35 G4
Dirty Mile CO CH5 .... 35 J6
Disraeli Cl CO CH5 .... 15 G6
Dock Rd CO CH5 .... 15 G6
Dodd's Dr CO CH5 .... 25 H1
Dol Awel CO CH5 .... 35 H1
Dolphin Ct CHSW/BR CH4 .... 39 G3
Donne Pl CH/BCN CH1 .... 29 G2
Donnation Wy CHSW/BR CH4 .... 39 F3
Dorchester Rd CHSW/BR CH4 .... 39 F3
Dorfold Wy CHNE CH2 .... 30 A2
Dormer Cl CHSE CH3 .... 41 J5
Dorset Pl CHSW/BR CH4 .... 30 C5
Dorset Rd CHNE CH2 .... 30 C5
Douglas Pl CHSW/BR CH4 .... 38 E4
Dover Rd CHSW/BR CH4 .... 39 G5
Dovey Cl CO CH5 .... 25 F2
  FLINT CH6 .... 13 F5
Downham Dr CHSE CH3 .... 41 J5
Downsfield Rd CHSW/BR CH4 .... 39 F4
Downswood Ct CH/BCN CH1 .... 17 J6
Dreflan MOLD/BUCK CH7 .... 42 E2
Drive A CO CH5 .... 16 E4
Drive B CO CH5 .... 16 E4
Drive C CO CH5 .... 16 E4
Drive D CO CH5 .... 16 E5
Drome Rd CO CH5 .... 16 E5
Drury La MOLD/BUCK CH7 .... 45 H5
  CHSE CH3 .... 50 A1
Drury New Rd
  MOLD/BUCK CH7 .... 35 G5
Dryden Cl CO CH5 .... 35 G2
Dryersfield CHSE CH3 .... 40 C2
Duckers La CO CH5 .... 26 C6
Duffryn Cl MOLD/BUCK CH7 .... 35 H1
Dukesfield Cl MOLD/BUCK CH7 ..... 35 G3
Duke's Field Dr
  MOLD/BUCK CH7 .... 34 E5
Duke St CH/BCN CH1 .... 2 E5
  FLINT CH6 .... 13 G3
Dukesway CHNE CH2 .... 30 A1
Dulas Ct CHNE CH2 .... 20 A6
Dulverton Av CHSE CH3 .... 30 C6
Dunbar Cl CO CH5 .... 15 F5
Dundas St CO CH5 .... 15 G6
Dunham Wy CHNE CH2 .... 30 D2
Dunlin Av CO CH5 .... 15 F6
Durban Av CHSE CH3 .... 30 C6
Durham Rd CH/BCN CH1 .... 29 F3
Dwyfor Av MOLD/BUCK CH7 .... 43 K2
Dyfed Dr CO CH5 .... 26 A4
Dylan Cl CO CH5 .... 35 G3
Dyserth Rd CH/BCN CH1 .... 28 D5

E

Eardswick Cl CHNE CH2 .... 29 K5
Earle's Crs CO CH5 .... 25 F1
Earl Rd (Heol yr Iarll)
  MOLD/BUCK CH7 .... 43 F3
Earls Oak CHNE CH2 .... 29 K1
Earls Port CH/BCN CH1 .... 2 B3
Earlston Ct CHSE CH3 .... 40 B4
Earl St FLINT CH6 .... 13 G2
Earlsway CHSW/BR CH4 .... 39 G3
East Cl MOLD/BUCK CH7 .... 43 J5
Eastern Pathway
  CH/BCN CH1 .... 3 G7
Eastfields Gv CH/BCN CH1 .... 18 A6
Eastgate Rw North
  CH/BCN CH1 .... 2 E4
Eastgate St CH/BCN CH1 .... 2 E4
Eastgate Rw South
  CH/BCN CH1 .... 2 E4
Eastgate St CH/BCN CH1 .... 2 E4
East Vw MOLD/BUCK CH7 .... 33 J6
Eaton Av CO CH5 .... 39 K3
  CO CH5 .... 25 H2
Eaton Cl CHSW/BR CH4 .... 38 E5
Eaton Ms CHSW/BR CH4 .... 39 K5
Eaton Rd CHSW/BR CH4 .... 39 K3
Ebury Pl CHSW/BR CH4 .... 39 K4
Eccleston Av CHSW/BR CH4 .... 39 K4
Eccleston Rd CHSW/BR CH4 .... 46 E5
Echo Cl CHSW/BR CH4 .... 38 E5
Edgar Pl CHSW/BR CH4 .... 2 E7
Edge Gv CHNE CH2 .... 30 A1
Edinburgh Wy WRX/GR/LL LL12 .... 51 H6
Edinburgh Wy CHSW/BR CH4 .... 3 H6
Edmund St MOLD/BUCK CH7 .... 43 F4
Edna St CHNE CH2 .... 3 J1
Edwards Rd CHSW/BR CH4 .... 39 J4
Edwin Dr FLINT CH6 .... 13 H4
Egerton Dr CHNE CH2 .... 29 K3
Egerton Rd CHNE CH2 .... 28 D3
Egerton St CH/BCN CH1 .... 3 G2
Egerton Wk CHSW/BR CH4 .... 48 A6
Eggbridge La CHSE CH3 .... 41 J5
Eglwys Cl MOLD/BUCK CH7 .... 34 C6
Elder Dr MOLD/BUCK CH7 .... 34 C4
Elfed Dr MOLD/BUCK CH7 .... 34 C6
Elgin Cl CHSE CH3 .... 30 C5
Elicle Cl CO CH5 .... 14 E6
Eliot Cl CO CH5 .... 35 H2
Elizabeth Crs CHSW/BR CH4 .... 3 H5
Ellesmere Av CHSW/BR CH4 ..... 29 K3
  CO CH5 .... 25 H4
Ellesmere Rd
  MOLD/BUCK CH7 .... 34 A6
Elm Av CO CH5 .... 25 F1
  FLINT CH6 .... 13 F5
Elm Cft CO CH5 .... 26 C6

Elm Dr MOLD/BUCK CH7 .... 24 B4
  MOLD/BUCK CH7 .... 42 E2
Elm Gv CHSW/BR CH4 .... 38 E5
Elm Rd CO CH5 .... 25 J5
Elm Sq CHSW/BR CH4 .... 39 F4
The Elms CO CH5 .... 35 H5
Elm Wk MOLD/BUCK CH7 .... 34 A5
Elm Wy CO CH5 .... 25 C6
Elmwood Av CHNE CH2 .... 30 B4
Elmwood Cl CO CH5 .... 25 K4
Elstree Av CHSE CH3 .... 30 D5
Elton St MOLD/BUCK CH7 .... 43 F4
Elwy Crs FLINT CH6 .... 13 F5
Embassy Cl CH/BCN CH1 .... 28 D3
Enderby Rd CH/BCN CH1 .... 2 C1
Endsleigh Cl CHNE CH2 .... 20 A6
Endsleigh Gdns CHNE CH2 .... 20 A6
Englefield Av CHSW/BR CH4 ..... 38 D4
  CO CH5 .... 25 H4
Englefield Cl MOLD/BUCK CH7 ... 43 K2
Englefield Dr FLINT CH6 .... 13 J4
Englefield Rd HLYW CH8 .... 5 G5
Ennerdale CHNE CH2 .... 30 B3
Erith St MOLD/BUCK CH7 .... 50 B2
Ermine Rd CHNE CH2 .... 30 A4
Erw Fach MOLD/BUCK CH7 .... 43 K1
Erw Goed MOLD/BUCK CH7 .... 20 A6
Essex Rd CHNE CH2 .... 30 C3
Estuary Vw CO CH5 .... 15 F5
Estyn Cl WRX/GR/LL LL12 .... 51 J5
Ethelda Dr CHNE CH2 .... 30 C3
Etna Rd MOLD/BUCK CH7 .... 50 A2
Etterick Dr CHSE CH3 .... 30 C6
Ettrick Pk CHSE CH3 .... 30 C6
Eurgain Av (Rhodfa Eurgain)
  CO CH5 .... 24 E2
Evansleigh Dr CO CH5 .... 15 F6
Evans St FLINT CH6 .... 13 G2
Eversley Cl CHNE CH2 .... 29 J4
Eversley Pk CHNE CH2 .... 29 J4
Ewart St CHSW/BR CH4 .... 38 B3
Ewloe Pl MOLD/BUCK CH7 .... 34 D4
Exeter Pl CH/BCN CH1 .... 29 F3
Exton Pk CH/BCN CH1 .... 29 F3

F

Factory Rd CO CH5 .... 26 D4
Fagl La WRX/GR/LL LL12 .... 51 G5
Fairfield Rd CHNE CH2 .... 30 C4
  CHSW/BR CH4 .... 37 F6
  CO CH5 .... 26 B3
  MOLD/BUCK CH7 .... 35 H5
Fairford Rd CHSW/BR CH4 .... 39 F4
Fairhaven HLYW CH8 .... 4 E2
Fairholme Cl CH/BCN CH1 .... 18 B5
Fairoaks Dr CO CH5 .... 26 C6
Fairview CHSW/BR CH4 .... 48 A6
Fairway Cl CO CH5 .... 26 E5
Fairway CO CH5 .... 26 E5
Fammau View Dr
  CHSW/BR CH4 .... 45 J3
Farbailey Cl CHSW/BR CH4 ...... 38 B3
Farfield Av CO CH5 .... 25 G1
Farm Cl MOLD/BUCK CH7 .... 34 C6
Farm La CHSW/BR CH4 .... 14 E5
Farmfield Cl CO CH5 .... 25 H6
Farm Rd CO CH5 .... 26 C1
  MOLD/BUCK CH7 .... 44 C1
Farndon Cl CHSW/BR CH4 .... 37 C6
Faulkners Cl CHSE CH3 .... 41 F5
Faulkner St CHNE CH2 .... 30 B5
Feathers La CH/BCN CH1 * 2 D5
Feathers St FLINT CH6 .... 13 G2
Fedwen Arian CHSW/BR CH4 ...... 45 J2
Feilden Ct CH/BCN CH1 .... 19 F5
Fellows La WRX/GR/LL LL12 ..... 51 J4
Fern Cl FLINT CH6 .... 13 F4
Ferndale Cl CHSW/BR CH4 .... 45 K3
Fernhill Rd CH/BCN CH1 .... 28 E2
Fernlea Ct CH/BCN CH1 .... 17 K6
Fernside Rd CO CH5 .... 25 J4
Ferry Bank (Glan y Fferi)
  CO CH5 .... 26 C2
Ferry Cl CO CH5 .... 26 E2
Ferry La CH/BCN CH1 .... 28 E5
Ffawydden MOLD/BUCK CH7 ...... 34 D5
Fford Babell HLYW CH8 .... 10 A1
Fford Bryn Estyn
  MOLD/BUCK CH7 .... 42 D3
Ffordd Argoed
  MOLD/BUCK CH7 .... 43 H2
Ffordd Argoed (Argoed Rd)
  MOLD/BUCK CH7 .... 34 D5
Ffordd Brenig
  MOLD/BUCK CH7 .... 34 A5
Ffordd Briggo
  MOLD/BUCK CH7 .... 34 A5
Ffordd Cae Llwyn CO CH5 ...... 35 G3
Ffordd Calcoed HLYW CH8 ...... 6 E6
Ffordd Celyn MOLD/BUCK CH7 ... 35 G3
Ffordd Derwyn CHSW/BR CH4 .... 50 A2
Ffordd Dol Goed
  MOLD/BUCK CH7 .... 42 E4
Ffordd Edwin
  MOLD/BUCK CH7 .... 23 G6
Ffordd Estyn MOLD/BUCK CH7 ... 43 K2
Ffordd Fer MOLD/BUCK CH7 ..... 43 K2
Ffordd Ffynnon CO CH5 .... 35 H2
Ffordd Glyn MOLD/BUCK CH7 .... 43 F4
Ffordd Glyndwr
  MOLD/BUCK CH7 .... 23 G6
Ffordd Gwynedd
  MOLD/BUCK CH7 .... 23 G6
Ffordd Hafod (Hafod Rd)
  MOLD/BUCK CH7 .... 42 A4
Ffordd Hengoed
  MOLD/BUCK CH7 .... 42 E4
Ffordd Kinderley CO CH5 ...... 25 F2

Ffordd Las CHSW/BR CH4 * 45
  MOLD/BUCK CH7 33
Ffordd Llanarth CO CH5 24
Ffordd Llaneurgain
  (Northop Rd) FLINT CH6 13
Ffordd Llanfynydd
  MOLD/BUCK CH7 50
Ffordd Llewelyn FLINT CH6 13
Ffordd Mellion CO CH5 24
Ffordd Newydd CO CH5 24
Ffordd Offa MOLD/BUCK CH7 43
Ffordd Ogwen
  MOLD/BUCK CH7 34
Ffordd Owen MOLD/BUCK CH7 25
Ffordd Pant Gwyn CO CH5 25
Ffordd Pel-y-Dryn CO CH5 35
Ffordd Pennant
  MOLD/BUCK CH7 42
Ffordd Pentre
  MOLD/BUCK CH7 43
Ffordd Pentre Bach
  MOLD/BUCK CH7 42
Ffordd Pen-y-Maes
  (Pen-y-Maes Rd) HLYW CH8 8
Ffordd Tegid CO CH5 35
Ffordd Trem y Foel
  MOLD/BUCK CH7 42
Ffordd Walwen HLYW CH8 10
Ffordd y Fran FLINT CH6 13
Ffordd y Goedwig (Forest Wk)
  MOLD/BUCK CH7 33
Fford Eidon MOLD/BUCK CH7 33
Fford Ganol MOLD/BUCK CH7 33
Fford Tirion MOLD/BUCK CH7 ... 33
Fiddlers La CHSE CH3 31
Field Cl FLINT CH6 18
Field Farm La MOLD/BUCK CH7 . 34
Field Farm Rd
  MOLD/BUCK CH7 34
Fielding Cl CO CH5 35
Field Rd MOLD/BUCK CH7 35
Fieldside CO CH5 36
Field Vw CO CH5 36
Fieldway CH/BCN CH1 18
  CHNE CH2 30
Fifth Av FLINT CH6 16
Filkin's La CHSE CH3 40
Finchett Dr CH/BCN CH1 2
Firbeck Cl CHSW/BR CH4 47
Fir-Brook Av CO CH5 26
Firbrook Av CO CH5 26
Firemans Sq CH/BCN CH1 * 2
First Av CO CH5 16
  FLINT CH6 13
The Firs MOLD/BUCK CH7 43
Fir Tree MOLD/BUCK CH7 39
Fir Tree La CHSE CH3 41
Fishermans' Rd CO CH5 15
Fisher Rd CH/BCN CH1 28
Five Ashes Rd CHSW/BR CH4 39
Flag La North CHNE CH2 21
Flaxfield Cl HLYW CH8 7
Flaxmere Dr CHSE CH3 40
Flookersbrook CHNE CH2 30
Florita Cl CO CH5 14
Foregate Cl CHSW/BR CH4 9
Forest Dr CHSW/BR CH4 47
Forest Cl CH/BCN CH1 3
Forest Wk (Ffordd y Goedwig)
  MOLD/BUCK CH7 35
Forge Wy CHSW/BR CH4 39
Fourth Av CO CH5 16
  FLINT CH6 13
Fowler Rd CH/BCN CH1 28
Foxcote Cl CH/BCN CH1 28
Fox Cover CHSE CH3 31
Fox Covert La CHNE CH2 20
Foxes Cl CO CH5 26
Foxes Wk CHSE CH3 46
Foxglove Cl CHSE CH3 40
Fox La CHSE CH3 41
Fox Lea CH/BCN CH1 18
Fox's Dr CO CH5 26
Foxwist Cl CHNE CH2 29
Francis Cl CH/BCN CH1 3
Francis St CH/BCN CH1 3
Fraser Cr CHSW/BR CH4 39
Fraser Dr MOLD/BUCK CH7 23
Friars Ct CO CH5 36
Frodsham Sq CH/BCN CH1 3
Frodsham St CH/BCN CH1 2
Fron Deg FLINT CH6 9
Fron Heulog CO CH5 35
Fron Las HLYW CH8 8
Fron Park Rd HLYW CH8 7
Fron Rd CO CH5 25
Fulbrooke HLYW CH8 5
Furne Rd CH/BCN CH1 18

G

Gadlys La FLINT CH6 9
Gainford Av CO CH5 29
Gala Cl CHSW/BR CH4 47
Gardd Eirlys MOLD/BUCK CH7 ... 34
Gardd Eithin MOLD/BUCK CH7 ... 24
Gardd-y-Gwanwyn
  MOLD/BUCK CH7 * 24
Garden Cl CH/BCN CH1 2
Garden La CH/BCN CH1 2
Garden Rw HLYW CH8 4
Garden Ter CHSE CH3 3
Garden Wy CO CH5 26
Garratt Cl CO CH5 25
Garth Dr CHNE CH2 29
Garth Ganol FLINT CH6 13
Garthorpe Av CO CH5 15
Garthorpe Cl CO CH5 15
Gas La (Lon Nwy)
  MOLD/BUCK CH7 43
Gateshealh Dr CHNE CH2 29
Gawer Pk CH/BCN CH1 29
Gaymoore Cl CHNE CH2 29

...yton Cl *CHNE* CH2 .... 30 A3
CQ CH5 .... 25 F2
...elli Dywod (Sandy Gv)
MOLD/BUCK CH7 .... 42 E4
...eorge St *CH/BCN* CH1 .... 2 D3
...errards Av *CHSE* CH3 .... 40 C1
...ry-Llan *MOLD/BUCK* CH7... .... 42 B5
...wern Cl *CH/BCN* CH1 .... 29 J4
...psy La *CH/BCN* CH1 .... 19 F4
...adstone Av *CQ* CH5 .... 25 K2
...adstone Rd *CH/BCN* CH1 .... 2 B1
CHSW/BR CH4 .... 47 F1
...adstone St *CQ* CH5 .... 25 J2
MOLD/BUCK CH7 .... 42 A5
...adstone Ter *CQ* CH5 .... 26 D5
...adstone Wy *CQ* CH5 .... 26 B6
...amis Cl *CHSE* CH3 .... 30 C6
...an Aber *MOLD/BUCK* CH7 * ...43 F3
...an Aber Pk *CHSW/BR* CH4 ...39 G3
...an Alun *MOLD/BUCK* CH7 ...43 F4
...an Gors *FLINT* CH6 .... 13 H5
...anafron Rd *MOLD/BUCK* CH7 ...43 F3
...an-y-Don *HLYW* CH8 .... 8 D1
...an y Fferi (Ferry Bank)
.... 26 C2
...an yr Eglwys
MOLD/BUCK CH7 * 23 C5
...asll Wyn *CQ* CH5 .... 25 K4
...astonbury Av *CHNE* CH2 ...30 B1
...ebe Mdw *CHNE* CH2 .... 21 H5
...eggs Cl *CHSE* CH3 .... 40 D5
...endale Av *CQ* CH5 .... 25 H3
...eneagles Cl *CHSE* CH3 .... 30 D5
...enesk Ct *CQ* CH5 .... 26 D2
...enside Ct *CH/BCN* CH1 .... 28 D3
...e Glen *CH/BCN* CH1 .... 28 E3
...obe Wy *MOLD/BUCK* CH7 ...34 E3
...oucester Av *CQ* CH5 .... 25 K2
...oucester St *CH/BCN* CH1 ...2 E1
...overs Loom *CHSE* CH3 .... 40 D5
...yn Abbott Avene *HLYW* CH8 ...8 B2
...yndwr Ct *MOLD/BUCK* CH7...43 C4
...ynnedale Pk *CQ* CH5 .... 35 J1
...ynne St *CQ* CH5 .... 25 H1
...ynne Wy *CQ* CH5 .... 36 B2
...ynteg *MOLD/BUCK* CH7 * ...43 F4
...yn Teg *MOLD/BUCK* CH7 ...43 F4
...dre'r Coed *MOLD/BUCK* CH7 ...42 B5
...dre'r Mynydd
MOLD/BUCK CH7 .... 42 C5
...dre'r Waen *FLINT* CH6 .... 23 C2
...dstall La *CH/BCN* CH1 .... 2 E4
...alftyn Dr *CQ* CH5 .... 14 E6
...alftyn La *CQ* CH5 .... 24 D1
...ansley Cl *CHNE* CH2 .... 29 K5
...odwood Gv
MOLD/BUCK CH7 .... 2 A2
...oodwood Gv
MOLD/BUCK CH7 .... 24 C4
...ordon Av *CQ* CH5 .... 50 A1
...ordon La *CHNE* CH2 .... 19 H1
...ordon Ter *MOLD/BUCK* CH7 * ...43 G2
...ornel Av *CQ* CH5 .... 25 G1
...orse Cl *CHSW/BR* CH4 .... 45 K3
...orse Stacks *CH/BCN* CH1 ...2 E3
...orse Wy *CHSE* CH3 .... 40 C5
...osforth Pl *CHNE* CH2 .... 30 B5
...smore Rd *MOLD/BUCK* CH7 ...34 C4
...ss St *CH/BCN* CH1 .... 2 D4
...wy Rd *CHNE* CH2 .... 21 H5
...ya Cl *CQ* CH5 .... 14 E6
...afton Ms *CHNE* CH2 .... 2 E1
...aham Rd *CH/BCN* CH1 .... 28 E3
...anby Ct *CQ* CH5 .... 25 F2
...ange La *HLYW* CH8 .... 7 H2
...ange Rd *CHNE* CH2 .... 29 K4
...... *CQ* CH5 .... 30 C6
CQ CH5 .... 35 J5
...angeside *CHNE* CH2 .... 29 K1
...anston Ct *CQ* CH5 .... 24 D4
...ant Dr *CQ* CH5 .... 25 J6
...anville Rd *CH/BCN* CH1 ...2 A1
...asmere Cl *CQ* CH5 .... 24 E1
...asmere Crs *MOLD/BUCK* CH7 ...35 F4
...asmere Rd *CHSE* CH3 .... 30 B3
...ays Rd *MOLD/BUCK* CH7 ...43 K3
...eenacre Dr *FLINT* CH6 .... 13 C6
...eenacre Rd *CHSW/BR* CH4 ...39 F6
...eenbank *CHSW/BR* CH4 ...40 A5
...eenbank Dr *FLINT* CH6 ...13 F4
...eenbank Rd *CHNE* CH2 .... 30 C6
CQ CH5 .... 25 J3
...eenbank Vls *FLINT* CH6 * ...13 C3
...eenfield Av *CQ* CH5 .... 46 E5
...eenfield Crs *CHSE* CH3 .... 30 D5
.... 61 A4
...eenfield La *CHNE* CH2 .... 21 J3
...eenfield Rd *CHSE* CH3 .... 41 K5
HLYW CH8 .... 37 C6
HLYW CH8 .... 8 A2
...eenfields *CHNEE* CH2 .... 29 F5
...eenfields La *CHSE* CH3 .... 41 H5
...eenhill Av *CQ* CH5 .... 35 J1
...een La *CH/BCN* CH1 .... 28 C2
...... *CHNE* CH2 .... 20 E3
CHSE CH3 .... 38 E5
CHSW/BR CH4 .... 46 E6
CHSE CH3 .... 34 E1
...een La East *CQ* CH5 .... 17 F4
...een Lane (West) *CH/BCN* CH1 ...17 F3
...een Mdw *CQ* CH5 .... 35 J2
...een Pk *CHSE* CH3 .... 45 J3
.... 25 H1
...eenside *MOLD/BUCK* CH7 ...42 E5
...eensway *CHSW/BR* CH4 ...39 G5
...e Green *CHSW/BR* CH4 ...47 F5
HLYW CH8 .... 10 B5
MOLD/BUCK CH7 .... 23 F6
...een Vls *CHSW/BR* CH4 * ...48 A5
...eenville Av *CQ* CH5 .... 25 C6
...eenway *CH/BCN* CH1 .... 18 A5
...eenway St *CHSW/BR* CH4 ...39 F3
...esford Av *CHNE* CH2 .... 30 A5
...esford Rd *WRX/CR/LL* LL12 ...51 K5
...ey Cl *CQ* CH5 .... 35 G2
...ey Friars *CH/BCN* CH1 ...2 C5
...eyhound Park Rd
CH/BCN CH1 .... 29 F5

Greystones Rd *CHSE* CH3 ...40 E1
Griffin Cl *CH/BCN* CH1 .... 29 F3
Griffiths Ct *CQ* CH5 .... 25 J3
Grindley Bank *CHNE* CH2 ...21 H6
Groomscroft *CQ* CH5 .... 35 K2
Groomsdale La *CQ* CH5 .... 35 K2
Grosvenor Dr *MOLD/BUCK* CH7 ...34 D5
Grosvenor Park Rd *CH/BCN* CH1 ...3 C4
Grosvenor Park Ter *CH/BCN* CH1... ...3 C5
Grosvenor Pl *CH/BCN* CH1 ...2 E6
Grosvenor Prec *CH/BCN* CH1 ...2 E4
Grosvenor Rd *CH/BCN* CH1 ...2 D7
CHSW/BR CH4 .... 39 J3
CQ CH5 .... 25 J2
Grosvenor Rbt *CH/BCN* CH1 ...2 D6
Grosvenor St *CH/BCN* CH1 ...2 D6
MOLD/BUCK CH7 .... 43 F3
Grove Av *CHSE* CH3 .... 30 D5
Grove Gdns *CHSE* CH3 .... 31 G6
Grove Rd *CH/BCN* CH1 .... 18 E1
The Groves *CH/BCN* CH1 ...3 C5
.... 24 B4
Guilden Gn *CHSE* CH3 .... 31 G3
Guilden Sutton La *CHSE* CH3 ...30 E4
Guildford Ct *CHSW/BR* CH4 ...39 F4
Guy La *CHSE* CH3 .... 41 K5
Gwalia *WRX/CR/LL* LL12 ...51 H6
Gwel Afon *HLYW* CH8 .... 7 J2
Gwel y Mynydd
MOLD/BUCK CH7 .... 34 C5
Gwenffrwd Rd *HLYW* CH8 ...7 K3
Gwernaffield Rd
MOLD/BUCK CH7 .... 42 D1
Gwylan Av *CQ* CH5 .... 15 G6
Gwynedd Dr *FLINT* CH6 ...13 G3

H

Hadfield Cl *CQ* CH5 .... 25 F3
Hadrian Dr *CH/BCN* CH1 ...28 E2
Hafan Deg *HLYW* CH8 .... 7 F1
Hafod Cl *CH/BCN* CH1 .... 28 D5
.... 14 E6
Hafod Dr *HLYW* CH8 .... 11 J4
Hafod Pk *CQ* CH5 .... 15 F6
Hafod Rd *MOLD/BUCK* CH7 ...42 A3
Hafod Rd (Ffordd Hafod)
MOLD/BUCK CH7 .... 42 A4
Hafod-y-Bryn *HLYW* CH8 ...7 J6
Hafod-y-Dolol Rd *HLYW* CH8 ...4 B2
Hafod-y-Wern
MOLD/BUCK CH7 .... 42 B5
Halkett Cl *CHSW/BR* CH4 ...38 E5
Halkyn Rd *CQ* CH5 .... 30 A5
FLINT CH6 .... 13 F6
HLYW CH8 .... 8 A3
Halkyn St *FLINT* CH6 .... 13 G3
Halkyn Vw *CQ* CH5 .... 25 F3
Hallfield Cl *FLINT* CH6 .... 13 F3
Hall La *CQ* CH5 .... 25 G2
Hall Vw *MOLD/BUCK* CH7 ...42 E1
Hals Cl *CQ* CH5 .... 14 E5
Halton Rd *CHSE* CH3 .... 30 E4
Hamilton Av *CQ* CH5 .... 26 E5
Hamilton Pl *CH/BCN* CH1 ...2 D4
Hamilton Rd *CQ* CH5 .... 15 F6
Hamilton St *CHNE* CH2 .... 30 B5
Hampton Av *CQ* CH5 .... 26 C4
Hampton Rd *CHSW/BR* CH4 ...39 F4
Hancock's La *CH/BCN* CH1 ...44 C1
Handbridge *CHSW/BR* CH4 ...2 E7
Handford Rd *CHNE* CH2 ...30 A2
Hanmer Ct *MOLD/BUCK* CH7 ...44 E1
Harbour Cl *FLINT* CH6 .... 30 A1
Harding Rd *CHNE* CH2 .... 19 H6
Harebell Cl *CHSE* CH3 .... 40 C4
Hare La *CHSE* CH3 .... 30 E4
Harington Cl *CHSE* CH3 .... 30 D5
Harington Rd *CHNE* CH2 ...19 J6
Harlech Av *CQ* CH5 .... 25 F1
Harlech Cl *MOLD/BUCK* CH7 ...34 E3
Harrison Cv *CQ* CH5 .... 14 E6
Harrowby Rd *MOLD/BUCK* CH7 ...43 F2
Hartford Wy *CH/BCN* CH1 ...29 C6
Harthill Rd *CHNE* CH2 .... 28 E2
Hartington St *CHSW/BR* CH4 ...40 A3
Hartley Cl *CHSW/BR* CH4 ...46 B6
Haslin Crs *CHSE* CH3 .... 41 F5
Hassals La *CHNE* CH2 .... 21 H3
Hatchmere Dr *CHSE* CH3 ...40 D2
Hatherton Wy *CHNE* CH2 ...29 K5
Hatton Rd *CH/BCN* CH1 ...28 E3
Haulfryn *MOLD/BUCK* CH7 ...33 G4
Hawarden Br *CQ* CH5 .... 26 A1
Hawarden Rd *CHSW/BR* CH4 ...45 J4
WRX/CR/LL LL12 .... 51 J5
Hawarden Wy *CQ* CH5 ...26 C6
Hawker Cl *CHSW/BR* CH4 ...37 C6
Hawkesbury Rd
MOLD/BUCK CH7 .... 34 D5
Hawklane Cl *CQ* CH5 .... 25 F1
Hawthorn Av *CQ* CH5 .... 42 E1
MOLD/BUCK CH7 .... 34 E6
Hawthorne Av
MOLD/BUCK CH7 .... 34 E6
Hawthorn Rd *CHSE* CH3 ...41 G3
CHSW/BR CH4 .... 39 F5
Hawthorn Vw *CQ* CH5 .... 26 E2
Haydan Ct *CHNE* CH2 .... 29 K4
Haydock Cl *CH/BCN* CH1 ...2 A2
Haydon Wy *CQ* CH5 .... 26 D2
Hayes Pk *CH/BCN* CH1 ...29 J5
Haymakers Cl *CHNE* CH2 ...39 F6
Haymakers Wy *CH/BCN* CH1 ...18 A6
Hazel Ct *FLINT* CH6 .... 12 E4
Hazel Dr *CHSW/BR* CH4 ...45 K3
Hazel Gv *MOLD/BUCK* CH7 ...42 E2
Hazel Rd *CHSW/BR* CH4 ...39 F5
WRX/CR/LL LL12 .... 51 H6
Hazelwood Cl *CQ* CH5 .... 25 F3
Hazelwood Crs *CQ* CH5 ...35 H5
The Headlands *CQ* CH5 ...3 C4
Health St *CQ* CH5 .... 25 K2

Heath Bank *CHSE* CH3 .... 31 F4
Heath Cl *CHSE* CH3 .... 40 D2
Heathcote Cl *CHNE* CH2 ...30 J4
Heather Ct *CHSE* CH3 .... 40 C2
Heathfields Cl *CHNE* CH2 ...29 K5
Heath La *CHSE* CH3 .... 40 C2
Heath Rd *CHNE* CH2 .... 29 K1
The Hedgerows *CQ* CH5 ...35 H1
Henblas *FLINT* CH6 .... 23 G2
Hendir *FLINT* CH6 .... 23 G2
Hendy Rd *MOLD/BUCK* CH7 ...42 B3
Henffordd *MOLD/BUCK* CH7 ...42 A5
Henley Av *CQ* CH5 .... 25 H2
Henley Rd *CHSW/BR* CH4 ...39 F4
Henrietta St *CQ* CH5 .... 25 K2
Henry Pl *CH/BCN* CH1 .... 2 E2
Henry Taylor St *FLINT* CH6 ...13 H2
Henry Wood Ct *CHSW/BR* CH4 ...38 E4
Henshall St *CH/BCN* CH1 ...2 B1
Heol Fammau
MOLD/BUCK CH7 .... 43 K1
Heol Tywysog *HLYW* CH8 ...11 J4
Heol-y-Bryn *FLINT* CH6 ...13 J5
Heol-y-Ddewaen
.... 50 A2
Heol y Goron *MOLD/BUCK* CH7 ...50 A2
Heol yr Iarll (Earl Rd)
.... 13 G3
Hereford Pl *CH/BCN* CH1 ...29 G4
Hereward Rd *CHSE* CH3 ...40 D1
Hermitage Ct *CHSW/BR* CH4 ...18 A6
Hermitage Rd *CHNE* CH2 ...37 F6
Heron Pl *CHNE* CH2 .... 37 F6
Herons Wy *CHSW/BR* CH4 ...49 G2
Herriot Gv *CQ* CH5 .... 35 G1
Heulwen Ct *WRX/CR/LL* LL12 ...51 J6
Hewitt's La *MOLD/BUCK* CH7 ...34 C6
Hewitt St *FLINT* CH6 .... 3 K1
Hey La *CQ* CH5 .... 35 C1
The Heywoods *CHNE* CH2 ...29 J4
Hickmore Heys *CHSE* CH3 ...31 H3
Highcliffe Av *CHNE* CH2 ...29 H4
Highcroft *CQ* CH5 .... 25 J3
The Highcroft *MOLD/BUCK* CH7 ...24 E2
Higher Cl *CQ* CH5 .... 25 J1
FLINT CH6 .... 9 G3
Higher Common Cl
MOLD/BUCK CH7 .... 34 E4
Higher Common Rd
MOLD/BUCK CH7 .... 34 E4
Higher Common Wy
MOLD/BUCK CH7 .... 34 E4
Highfield Ct *CQ* CH5 .... 36 A2
Highfield Av *MOLD/BUCK* CH7 ...42 B5
Highfield Rd *MOLD/BUCK* CH7 ...44 E1
Highfield Rd *CH/BCN* CH1 ...28 D3
FLINT CH6 .... 9 C4
Highfield Vls *MOLD/BUCK* CH7 ...43 F4
Highland Av *CQ* CH5 .... 25 J3
High Meadow Ct *CQ* CH5 ...11 F3
High Meadow Ct (Llys
Maes Ucha) *FLINT* CH6 * ...13 F3
High Pk *CQ* CH5 .... 36 A1
High St *CHSW/BR* CH4 ...25 J1
FLINT CH6 .... 9 G3
MOLD/BUCK CH7 .... 23 G6
MOLD/BUCK CH7 .... 43 F3
WRX/CR/LL LL12 .... 51 H6
Highvale *CQ* CH5 .... 24 E1
The Highway *CQ* CH5 .... 35 J1
Hilary Cl *CHSE* CH3 .... 40 D1
Hilbre Rd *CQ* CH5 .... 15 F6
Hilary Gv *MOLD/BUCK* CH7 ...34 D6
Hillcourt Av *FLINT* CH6 .... 9 J6
Hillsdown Dr *CQ* CH5 .... 24 E1
Hillside Cl *CQ* CH5 .... 25 F1
Hillside Ct *HLYW* CH8 .... 4 B2
Hillside Crs *MOLD/BUCK* CH7 ...34 E6
MOLD/BUCK CH7 .... 42 E1
CHSW/BR CH4 .... 38 E4
Hillside Rd *CH/BCN* CH1 ...28 E4
CHSW/BR CH4 .... 45 J3
Hillside Wy *CHNE* CH2 ...13 F4
Hillsview Rd *MOLD/BUCK* CH7 ...34 D6
Hilltop Cl *CQ* CH5 .... 25 G6
Hilltop Rd *CHSE* CH3 .... 31 H3
Hill Vw *MOLD/BUCK* CH7 ...34 D6
Hoel-y-Wern *MOLD/BUCK* CH7 ...42 B5
Holbein Cl *CHSW/BR* CH4 ...39 K4
The Holkham *CHSE* CH3 ...34 E4
The Hollies *MOLD/BUCK* CH7 ...34 E4
Hollins La *CQ* CH5 .... 35 H3
Hollowbrook Dr *CQ* CH5 ...24 E2
Holly Cl *CHNE* CH2 .... 21 H6
.... 14 E5
MOLD/BUCK CH7 .... 34 E6
Holly Ct *MOLD/BUCK* CH7 ...50 A1
Holly Dr *CHSW/BR* CH4 ...45 K3
.... 42 E2
Holly Gv *CQ* CH5 .... 25 K5
Holly Rd *CHSW/BR* CH4 ...39 F5
Holme Cl *CHSE* CH3 .... 41 G3
Holway Rd *HLYW* CH8 .... 7 H1
Holy Gra *CQ* CH5 .... 24 E1
Holyrood Wy *CHSE* CH3 ...30 D5
Holywell Rd *CQ* CH5 .... 25 G5
FLINT CH6 .... 13 G2
Holywell St *FLINT* CH6 ...13 G2
Home Pk *CH/BCN* CH1 ...19 F5
Honeysuckle Cl *CHSW/BR* CH4 ...47 G1
Hoole Br *CHNE* CH2 .... 30 B4
Hoole Gdns *CHNE* CH2 ...30 D5
Hoole La *CHNE* CH2 .... 3 J1
Hoole Pk *CHNE* CH2 .... 30 D4
Hoole Rd *CHNE* CH2 .... 3 J1
Hoole Wy *CH/BCN* CH1 ...3 F2
Hoole Way Rbt *CH/BCN* CH1 ...3 F2
Hope Bar Dr *WRX/CR/LL* LL12 ...51 J5
Hope Rd *CHSE* CH3 .... 47 F1
Hope St *CHSW/BR* CH4 ...39 F5
WRX/CR/LL LL12 .... 51 H6
Hope View Ct *MOLD/BUCK* CH7 ...34 E5
Hornbeam Av *MOLD/BUCK* CH7 ...34 E5
Hornesby Ct *CQ* CH5 .... 14 E6
Horrocks Rd *CHNE* CH2 ...30 A3

Hough Gn *CHSW/BR* CH4 ...39 G4
Houghton Cl *CHNE* CH2 ...3 K2
Housesteads Dr *CHNE* CH2 ...3 K1
Housman Cl *CH/BCN* CH1 ...29 C5
Howard Rd *CHSW/BR* CH4 ...38 D4
Howards Cl *CHSW/BR* CH4 ...45 J4
Howard St *CQ* CH5 .... 25 H1
Howe Rd *CHSW/BR* CH4 ...39 K3
Hugh St *CHSW/BR* CH4 ...39 K3
Hulleys Cl *CHSW/BR* CH4 ...39 F5
Hunters Cl *CHSW/BR* CH4 ...46 D5
Hunter St *CH/BCN* CH1 ...2 D4
Hunters Wk *CH/BCN* CH1 ...2 D4
Hunts Cl *CHSE* CH3 .... 40 D1
Hurbutts Dr *CQ* CH5 .... 26 A2
Hurlestone Cl *CHNE* CH2 ...21 H5
Hurstwood *CHSE* CH3 .... 41 J6
Huxleys La *WRX/CR/LL* LL12 ...51 J4

I

Imperial Av *CH/BCN* CH1 ...28 C4
Ince La *CHNE* CH2 .... 21 K4
Ingham Cl *CHSE* CH3 .... 40 C1
Institute La *MOLD/BUCK* CH7 ...34 C4
Irving's Crs *CHSW/BR* CH4 ...38 D4
Isabella Ct *CHSW/BR* CH4 ...38 E4
Isglan Rd *HLYW* CH8 .... 4 B5
Is y Coed *MOLD/BUCK* CH7 ...50 A1
Iver Rd *CHNE* CH2 .... 30 A1
Ivy Crs *MOLD/BUCK* CH7 ...42 E2
Ivy Ms *MOLD/BUCK* CH7 ...30 C3

J

James Pl *CHNE* CH2 .... 3 K2
James St *CHNE* CH2 .... 3 F2
Jamieson Cl *CHSE* CH3 ...30 B6
Jasmine Crs *MOLD/BUCK* CH7 ...42 E2
Jenard Ct *HLYW* CH8 .... 10 B5
Jesmond Rd *CH/BCN* CH1 ...2 A2
Johnsons Cl *CHSE* CH3 ...39 H5
Jonathan's Wy *CHSE* CH3 ...28 E3
Jubilee Br *MOLD/BUCK* CH7 ...34 C5
Jubilee St *CQ* CH5 .... 25 K2
Julius Cl *FLINT* CH6 .... 13 J4
Juniper Cl *CQ* CH5 .... 25 F1
Juniper Ct *CHNE* CH2 .... 25 F1
Jupiter Dr *CH/BCN* CH1 ...28 E6

K

Kaleyards *CH/BCN* CH1 ...2 E1
Kearsley Av *CQ* CH5 .... 35 J1
Keats Cl *CQ* CH5 .... 35 J1
Kelsterton Ct *CQ* CH5 .... 14 E5
Kelsterton La *MOLD/BUCK* CH7 ...34 B2
Kelsterton Rd *FLINT* CH6 ...14 D5
Kelvin Gv *CHNE* CH2 .... 30 A4
Kempton Cl *CH/BCN* CH1 ...2 A2
Kendal Cl *CHNE* CH2 .... 30 C2
Kennedy Cl *CHNE* CH2 ...26 B6
Kennedy Dr *CQ* CH5 .... 25 K3
Kensington Crs *CQ* CH5 ...26 C6
Kensington Gn *CHSW/BR* CH4 ...39 F4
Kent Av *CQ* CH5 .... 25 K3
Kent Cl *CHSW/BR* CH4 ...45 K3
Kent Rd *CHNE* CH2 .... 30 C2
.... 15 F6
Keristal Av *CHSE* CH3 .... 40 C3
Kestrel Cl *CQ* CH5 .... 25 F3
Keswick Cl *CHNE* CH2 ...30 C3
Ketland Cl *CQ* CH5 .... 25 K2
Killins La *CQ* CH5 .... 15 F6
Kilmorey Park Av *CHNE* CH2 ...30 A5
Kilmorey Park Rd *CHNE* CH2 ...30 B5
Kiln Cl *MOLD/BUCK* CH7 ...34 C5
Kiln La *MOLD/BUCK* CH7 ...34 C5
Kiln Cl Lon Odyni *FLINT* CH6 ...13 G3
Kiln La *WRX/CR/LL* LL12 ...51 K5
Kimberley Ter *CHNE* CH2 ...3 K3
King Edward Br *FLINT* CH6 ...13 C4
King Edward St *CQ* CH5 ...25 J2
King George St *CQ* CH5 ...25 J2
Kings Av *FLINT* CH6 .... 13 H4
HLYW CH8 .... 5 G6
Kingsbury Cl *FLINT* CH6 ...12 E3
Kings Cl *CHNE* CH2 .... 39 F5
King's Crs East *CHSE* CH3 ...40 C1
King's Crs West *CHSE* CH3 ...40 C1
Kingsfield Ct *CHSW/BR* CH4 ...49 J1
Kingsley Gdns *CHSE* CH3 ...40 D2
Kingsley Rd *CHSE* CH3 ...40 D2
.... 26 D1
Kingsley Ter *CQ* CH5 * ...30 D6
Kingsmead *CHNE* CH2 ...29 J1
Kings Rd *CQ* CH5 .... 15 F6
Kingston Ct *CH/BCN* CH1 ...18 E4
Kingston Dr *CQ* CH5 .... 26 D6
King St *CH/BCN* CH1 .... 2 D7
MOLD/BUCK CH7 .... 43 F2
MOLD/BUCK CH7 .... 50 B1
Kingsway *CHNE* CH2 .... 30 A4
CQ CH5 .... 25 J2
WRX/CR/LL LL12 .... 51 K6
Kingsway West *CHNE* CH2 ...30 A4
Kingswood Av *CH/BCN* CH1 ...18 C6
Kingswood La *CH/BCN* CH1 ...18 C6
Kinnerton Cl *CHSW/BR* CH4 ...38 D5
Kinnerton Hts *CHSW/BR* CH4 ...46 E5
Kinnerton La *CHSW/BR* CH4 ...46 E5
Kinnerton Rd *WRX/CR/LL* LL12 ...51 J4
Kipling Cl *CQ* CH5 .... 35 G2
Kipling Rd *CHNE* CH2 ...29 F3
Kirby Cl *CHSE* CH3 .... 29 K3
Kirkby St *CHSW/BR* CH4 ...39 F5
Kirkwood Cl *CHSE* CH3 ...30 C6
Kitchen St *CH/BCN* CH1 ...2 B5
Knightsbridge Ct *CHNE* CH2 ...3 K5
Knights Gn *FLINT* CH6 .... 13 C3
Knowle La *MOLD/BUCK* CH7 ...34 E5

Knowsley Rd *CHNE* CH2 ...30 C4
Knutsford Wy *CH/BCN* CH1 ...29 F6
Kohima Crs *CQ* CH5 .... 40 D5
Kynaston Dr *CHSW/BR* CH4 ...38 C5

L

Laburnum Gv *CHSW/BR* CH4 ...38 D4
Lache Hall Crs *CHSW/BR* CH4 ...39 F6
Lache La *CHSW/BR* CH4 ...48 C3
Lache Park Av *CHSW/BR* CH4 ...39 G4
Lakeside *CHSW/BR* CH4 ...49 G2
Lakeside Cl *FLINT* CH6 .... 30 A1
MOLD/BUCK CH7 .... 34 D3
Lakewood *CHSW/BR* CH4 ...49 H2
Lamb's La *MOLD/BUCK* CH7 ...34 D3
Lancaster Dr *CHSE* CH3 ...30 D6
Lancaster Pk *CHSW/BR* CH4 ...46 E1
Langdale Av *CHSE* CH3 ...35 F5
Langford Crs *MOLD/BUCK* CH7 ...34 D3
Langport Dr *CHSE* CH3 ...30 E6
Lansdowne Gv *CHSW/BR* CH4 ...39 G3
Lansdowne Rd *CQ* CH5 ...35 J5
Lansdown Rd *CHSW/BR* CH4 ...47 F1
Larch Av *CQ* CH5 .... 25 K4
The Larches *CQ* CH5 .... 35 K5
Larchfields *CH/BCN* CH1 ...18 A6
Larch Wy *CHSW/BR* CH4 ...39 F5
Larksfield Cl *WRX/CR/LL* LL12 ...51 J5
Larkspur Cl *CHSW/BR* CH4 ...39 F6
Larne Dr *CHSW/BR* CH4 ...37 H6
Laurel Dr *MOLD/BUCK* CH7 ...34 E6
Laurel Gv *CHNE* CH2 .... 30 C5
Lavender Ct *CQ* CH5 .... 25 K2
Lawn Dr *CHNE* CH2 .... 29 K1
Lawnt-y-Pentre *FLINT* CH6 ...23 C2
Lawrence St *CQ* CH5 .... 26 E5
Laws Gdns *CHSE* CH5 .... 40 C2
Law St *CHNE* CH2 .... 3 K3
Leaches La *CQ* CH5 .... 26 C5
Leadbrook Dr *FLINT* CH6 ...13 K5
Lead Mills *FLINT* CH6 .... 43 G2
Lea Dr *MOLD/BUCK* CH7 ...34 E6
Leawood La *CH/BCN* CH1 ...3 C3
Lea Hall Pk *CHNE* CH2 ...19 C5
Leahurst Cl *CHNE* CH2 ...30 B4
Leaside Rd *CH/BCN* CH1 ...28 E2
Leasowe Ter
MOLD/BUCK CH7 * ...24 C4
.... 35 J4
Ledsham La *CQ* CH5 .... 25 K6
Leen La *CH/BCN* CH1 .... 2 D4
Leeswood Rd *MOLD/BUCK* CH7 ...34 D6
Leicester La *CHSW/BR* CH4 ...40 D6
Leighton Ct (Cwrt Leighton)
CQ CH5 .... 15 G6
Leonard St *CH/BCN* CH1 ...2 B1
Level Rd *CQ* CH5 .... 35 H2
Lexham Green Cl
MOLD/BUCK CH7 .... 34 E6
Leyfield Ct *CHSW/BR* CH4 ...39 F5
Leyland Dr *CHSW/BR* CH4 ...38 B4
Lichfield Rd *CHNE* CH2 ...29 F3
Lightfoot St *CHNE* CH2 ...3 H1
Lilac Dr *CHSW/BR* CH4 ...45 J4
Lime Cl *CQ* CH5 .... 24 E1
Lime Gv *CHNE* CH2 .... 30 B5
CHSE CH3 .... 38 D4
Lime Wood Cl *CHNE* CH2 ...30 C3
Lincoln Dr *CHNE* CH2 ...30 C3
Lincoln Rd *CH/BCN* CH1 ...29 F5
CQ CH5 .... 25 J6
Lindale Cl *CQ* CH5 .... 24 E4
Linden Av *CQ* CH5 .... 15 F6
Linden Dr *CHNE* CH2 ...21 H5
CQ CH5 .... 42 D4
Linden Gv *CHNE* CH2 ...30 C4
CHSE CH3 .... 38 D4
Linderick Av *MOLD/BUCK* CH7 ...34 C5
Lindfields *CHSW/BR* CH4 ...38 E3
Lindum Cl *MOLD/BUCK* CH7 ...33 J6
Linen Hall Pl *CH/BCN* CH1 * ...2 D5
Linkswway *CHNE* CH2 .... 29 J1
Linthorpe Cl *MOLD/BUCK* CH7 ...34 E6
Linthorpe Gdns
.... 34 E5
Linthorpe Rd *MOLD/BUCK* CH7 ...34 E6
Linwood Cl *CHSW/BR* CH4 ...45 K3
Little Abbey Gtwy *CH/BCN* CH1 ...2 D3
Little Heath Cl *CHSE* CH3 ...41 G2
Little Heath Rd *CHSE* CH3 ...41 G1
Little Mountain Rd
MOLD/BUCK CH7 .... 45 H1
Little Rake La *CHNE* CH2 ...19 K1
Little Roodee *CQ* CH5 .... 40 C1
Little St John St *CH/BCN* CH1 * ...3 C5
Littleton La *CHSE* CH3 .... 31 F6
Liverpool Rd *CH/BCN* CH1 ...19 H2
.... 2 D1
.... 25 H6
MOLD/BUCK CH7 .... 34 E5
Llandore Cl *CQ* CH5 .... 24 E4
Lleprog La *HLYW* CH8 .... 12 A2
Llewellyn St *CQ* CH5 .... 25 J2
Llewelyn Dr *MOLD/BUCK* CH7 ...34 A4
Lloyd Pl *CH/BCN* CH1 ...28 E4
Lloyd St *FLINT* CH6 .... 13 H2
Llwyn Alun *WRX/CR/LL* LL12 ...51 J5
Llwyn Bach *MOLD/BUCK* CH7 ...42 D4
Llwyn Clwyd *CQ* CH5 .... 25 K4
Llwyn Derw *MOLD/BUCK* CH7 ...43 K1
Llwyn Eglwys
WRX/CR/LL LL12 .... 51 J5
Llwyn Eithin *MOLD/BUCK* CH7 ...42 E4
Llwyn Helig (Willow Gv)
MOLD/BUCK CH7 .... 34 C3
Llwyni Dr *CQ* CH5 .... 24 E4
Llwyn-Ifor La *HLYW* CH8 ...4 B5
Llwyn Onn *MOLD/BUCK* CH7 ...34 A5
Llwyn Onn *FLINT* CH6 .... 23 H1
Llwyn Onn La *MOLD/BUCK* CH7 ...23 H1
Llys Alyn *CQ* CH5 .... 25 K4
Llys Ambrose *MOLD/BUCK* CH7 ...42 D4
Llys Argoed *MOLD/BUCK* CH7 ...43 K2
Llys Ben *MOLD/BUCK* CH7 ...24 C4
Llys Berllan *MOLD/BUCK* CH7 ...34 B5
Llys Brenig *CQ* CH5 .... 35 G2

Llys Cadnant (Cadnant Ct)
  CHSW/BR CH4 .... 37 H5
Llys Caer *CHSW/BR* CH4 .... 46 E1
Llys Cae'r Glo *MOLD/BUCK* CH7 ... 33 G4
Llys Ceibren *CQ* CH5 .... 25 K3
Llys Daniel Owen
  MOLD/BUCK CH7 .... 42 E1
Llys Dedwydd *HLYW* CH8 .... 11 H3
  MOLD/BUCK CH7 .... 43 K2
Llys Derwen *CHSW/BR* CH4 .... 46 D4
Llys Eithin *MOLD/BUCK* CH7 .... 24 C4
Llys Enfys *MOLD/BUCK* CH7 .... 22 A5
Llys Fammau *MOLD/BUCK* CH7 ...... 43 K2
Llys Gwynant *MOLD/BUCK* CH7 ..... 34 A4
Llys Helyg (Willow Cl)
  MOLD/BUCK CH7 .... 35 G6
Llys Maesteg *HLYW* CH8 .... 8 D1
Llys Maes Ucha (High
  Meadow Ct) *FLINT* CH6 * 13 F3
Llys Mai *MOLD/BUCK* CH7 .... 34 C5
Llys Menden *MOLD/BUCK* CH7 .... 42 D5
Llys Mervyn *MOLD/BUCK* CH7 .... 43 G4
Llys Nercwys *MOLD/BUCK* CH7 ...... 43 G4
Llys Padarn *CQ* CH5 .... 35 G2
Llys Pant Derw *CQ* CH5 .... 24 E2
Llys Pont y Garreg
  MOLD/BUCK CH7 .... 43 G3
Llys Preswylfa
  MOLD/BUCK CH7 .... 43 G3
Llys Sant Iago *CQ* CH5 .... 15 F5
Llys Tudela *MOLD/BUCK* CH7 .... 43 H5
Llys Wyrfa *MOLD/BUCK* CH7 .... 43 K2
Llys y Craig *MOLD/BUCK* CH7 .... 43 K1
Llys y Faenol *CQ* CH5 .... 37 F5
Llys y Foel *MOLD/BUCK* CH7 .... 42 D3
Llys-y-Fron *MOLD/BUCK* CH7 .... 42 D5
Llys-y-Nant *HLYW* CH8 .... 11 J4
  MOLD/BUCK CH7 .... 43 G4
Llys-y-Penglyn *FLINT* CH6 .... 23 F2
Llys-yr-Awel *MOLD/BUCK* CH7 * 43 G4
Llys yr Coed *MOLD/BUCK* CH7 .... 43 G5
Llys y Wennol *MOLD/BUCK* CH7 ..... 34 C4
Llys-y-Wern *MOLD/BUCK* CH7 .... 33 G4
Lodge Gdns *CHNE* CH2 .... 29 K2
Lodge La *CH/BCN* CH1 .... 14 A4
Lon Cae Del *CQ* CH5 .... 35 H2
  MOLD/BUCK CH7 .... 42 D3
Lon Celyn *CQ* CH5 .... 25 F1
Lon Dderwen *CQ* CH5 .... 25 F1
London Rd *MOLD/BUCK* CH7 .... 33 G4
Longacre Dr *FLINT* CH6 .... 9 H5
Longburgh Cl *CHNE* CH2 .... 3 K1
Longdale Dr *CH/BCN* CH1 .... 28 C3
Longfellow Av *CQ* CH5 .... 35 G2
Longfield Av *CHNE* CH2 .... 30 A1
Long La *CH/BCN* CH1 .... 18 B4
  CHNE CH2 .... 30 B1
Lon Goed *HLYW* CH8 .... 7 H2
Lon Groes *FLINT* CH6 .... 13 F5
Longster Trail *CHSE* CH3 .... 31 G4
Lon Gwynant *CQ* CH5 .... 35 G2
Lon Isaf *MOLD/BUCK* CH7 .... 43 G3
Lon Llwyni *CQ* CH5 .... 24 E5
Lon Nwy (Gas La)
  MOLD/BUCK CH7 .... 43 G3
Lon Odyn (Kiln Cl) *FLINT* CH6 .... 13 G3
Lonsdale Ct *CHSW/BR* CH4 .... 39 F6
Lon y Becws *FLINT* CH6 .... 13 G3
Lon-y-Berth *MOLD/BUCK* CH7 .... 42 D4
Lon-y-Coeg *MOLD/BUCK* CH7 .... 42 E4
Lon y Mynydd *HLYW* CH8 .... 7 G5
Lon-y-Plas *FLINT* CH6 .... 23 F1
Lon yr Orsaf *MOLD/BUCK* CH7 .... 42 E4
Lord St *CHSE* CH3 .... 3 K4
Louise St *CH/BCN* CH1 .... 2 C2
Love La *MOLD/BUCK* CH7 .... 43 F2
Love St *CH/BCN* CH1 .... 3 F4
Lower Aston Hall La *CQ* CH5 .... 25 K5
Lower Bridge St *CH/BCN* CH1 .... 2 E5
Lower Brook St *CQ* CH5 .... 15 F5
Lower Dee View Rd *HLYW* CH8 .... 5 F6
Lower Field Rd *CHSW/BR* CH4 .... 39 G5
Lower Mountain Rd
  MOLD/BUCK CH7 .... 45 K5
  WRX/CR/LL LL12 .... 51 K2
Lower Mumforth St
  FLINT CH6 * 13 H2
Lower Park Rd *CHNE* CH2 .... 29 G3
Lower Sydney St *FLINT* CH6 .... 13 H2
Lucerne Cl *CHSE* CH3 .... 40 D4
Ludlow Rd *CH/BCN* CH1 * 29 G3
Ludwell Cl *CHSW/BR* CH4 .... 39 H5
Lumley Rd *CH/BCN* CH1 * 3 F5
Lumley Rd *CHNE* CH2 .... 29 J4
Lupin Dr *CHSE* CH3 .... 40 D4
Lyme Gv *MOLD/BUCK* CH7 .... 45 K5
Lynfield Cl *CQ* CH5 .... 25 F1
Lynton Cl *CHSW/BR* CH4 * 39 F4
Lynton Pl *CHSW/BR* CH4 .... 39 F5
Lynwood Rd *CH/BCN* CH1 .... 29 F3
Lyon St *CH/BCN* CH1 .... 3 F2
Lyons Yd *CQ* CH5 .... 26 C4

M

Machynlleth Wy *CQ* CH5 .... 24 E2
Madeley Cl *CHSW/BR* CH4 .... 37 G6
Maelor Cl *MOLD/BUCK* CH7 .... 43 K2
Maengwyn Av *CQ* CH5 .... 24 E1
Maes Afon *FLINT* CH6 .... 13 F3
Maes Alaw *HLYW* CH8 .... 13 H4
  MOLD/BUCK CH7 .... 42 E5
Maes Bodlonfa
  MOLD/BUCK CH7 .... 42 E5
Maes Celyn *MOLD/BUCK* CH7 .... 23 F5
Maes Cynfaen *HLYW* CH8 .... 7 H5
Maes Deri *CQ* CH5 .... 35 H1
Maes Glanrafon
  MOLD/BUCK CH7 * 43 F1
Maes Glas *CQ* CH5 .... 15 F3
  FLINT CH6 .... 13 F3
Maes Gwalia *MOLD/BUCK* CH7 ...... 33 H4
Maes Gwelfor *HLYW* CH8 .... 11 H3
Maes Gwern *MOLD/BUCK* CH7 .... 42 E5

Maes Gwyn *FLINT* CH6 .... 13 J4
Maes-Hyfryd *FLINT* CH6 .... 13 G4
Maes Llwyfen *CQ* CH5 .... 25 K4
Maes Lygan *HLYW* CH8 .... 11 H4
Maes Pinwydd *CQ* CH5 .... 35 H1
Maes Teg *FLINT* CH6 .... 13 C5
Maes Uchaf *CQ* CH5 .... 24 E4
Maes Wepre *CQ* CH5 .... 25 G2
Maes y Berllan *CQ* CH5 .... 25 G2
Maes-y-Coed *CHSW/BR* CH4 .... 38 E4
  FLINT CH6 .... 13 F4
Maes-y-Dre Av *FLINT* CH6 .... 13 H4
Maes-y-Dyffryn *HLYW* CH8 * 5 G6
Maes y March *MOLD/BUCK* CH7 .... 42 E2
Maes y Meillion
  MOLD/BUCK CH7 .... 50 A2
Maes-y-Plwm *HLYW* CH8 * 7 H1
Maes-yr-Afon *HLYW* CH8 * 5 G6
Maes-yr-Haf
  MOLD/BUCK CH7 * 42 E3
Maes y Haul
  MOLD/BUCK CH7 .... 42 E4
Maes yr Odyn *HLYW* CH8 * 8 A3
Maes y Ysgol *FLINT* CH6 .... 13 F3
Maes y Twr *MOLD/BUCK* CH7 .... 43 G5
Magazine La *MOLD/BUCK* CH7 ...... 24 B5
Main Rd *MOLD/BUCK* CH7 .... 46 C6
  MOLD/BUCK CH7 .... 53 G4
Mainwaring Dr *CHSW/BR* CH4 .... 38 C3
Maitland Wy *CH/BCN* CH1 .... 28 D4
Makepeace Cl *CHSE* CH3 .... 30 C5
Mallory Wk *CHSW/BR* CH4 .... 48 A5
Mallow Cl *CHSE* CH3 .... 40 C4
Maltra Rd *CHNE* CH2 .... 19 H5
Malvern Rd *CH/BCN* CH1 .... 29 G4
Manbry Cl *CQ* CH5 .... 24 E1
Mancot La *CQ* CH5 .... 26 B5
Mancot Royal Ct *CQ* CH5 .... 26 B5
Mancot Wy *CQ* CH5 .... 26 C5
Manley Ct *CQ* CH5 .... 25 K1
Mannings La *CHNE* CH2 .... 20 E5
Mannings La South *CHNE* CH2 .... 30 C3
Manor Cl *CQ* CH5 .... 37 G3
Manor Crs *CQ* CH5 .... 37 G3
  CHSE CH3 .... 40 D1
  FLINT CH6 .... 9 J6
Manor Dr *CHSE* CH3 .... 34 E6
Manor Farm Cl *CHNE* CH2 .... 21 G6
Manor Flds *CHSW/BR* CH4 .... 36 E4
Manor Pk *MOLD/BUCK* CH7 .... 33 G4
Manor Rd *CHSW/BR* CH4 .... 39 H5
  CQ CH5 .... 26 E2
Maple Crs *CQ* CH5 .... 35 H3
Maple Cv *CHSE* CH3 .... 30 A4
  CHSW/BR CH4 .... 38 D5
Maplewood Gv *CH/BCN* CH1 .... 18 B6
Mapplewood Av *CQ* CH5 .... 26 D1
Marbury Av *MOLD/BUCK* CH7 .... 44 E1
Marbury Rd *CHSE* CH3 .... 30 C5
Marches Wy *CHSW/BR* CH4 .... 2 E3
Mare Hey La *CQ* CH5 .... 24 B3
Marfield Cl *FLINT* CH6 .... 13 H5
Marian *FLINT* CH6 .... 13 G5
Marian Dr *CHSE* CH3 .... 40 A3
Marina Dr *CHSW/BR* CH4 .... 30 A1
  CQ CH5 .... 25 K2
Mark Cl *CHNE* CH2 .... 3 K2
Market Sq *FLINT* CH6 .... 13 H2
Marlborough Av *CQ* CH5 .... 35 J2
Marlt Cft *CHSE* CH3 .... 40 D3
Marley Wy *CHSW/BR* CH4 .... 38 E3
Marl Heys *CHNE* CH2 .... 3 J2
Marlow Av *CHNE* CH2 .... 30 B1
Marlowe Av *CQ* CH5 .... 35 H2
Marlowe Cl *CH/BCN* CH1 .... 29 G3
Marston Av *CHSW/BR* CH4 .... 39 G4
Marston Cl *CHSW/BR* CH4 * 48 E5
Marlwood Pl *CHSW/BR* CH4 .... 48 A6
Marmel Dr *CQ* CH5 .... 26 C4
Marsh La *FLINT* CH6 .... 13 H5
Marsh Vw *CQ* CH5 .... 25 J1
Martin Cl *CHNE* CH2 .... 19 J4
Martin Rd *CHNE* CH2 .... 19 J6
Marton Rd *CHSW/BR* CH4 .... 47 C1
Masefield Dr *CH/BCN* CH1 .... 28 E2
Mason St *FLINT* CH6 .... 2 D2
Matthew Cl *CHNE* CH2 .... 3 K2
Maude St *CQ* CH5 .... 25 H1
Maxwell Av *CQ* CH5 .... 26 B5
Maxwell Cl *MOLD/BUCK* CH7 .... 50 A1
Maxwell Dr *MOLD/BUCK* CH7 .... 50 A1
Maydor Av *CHSW/BR* CH4 .... 48 E6
Mayfield Dr *MOLD/BUCK* CH7 .... 34 B6
Mayfield Ms *MOLD/BUCK* CH7 ...... 34 C5
Mayfield Rd *CH/BCN* CH1 .... 28 D3
Maytree Av *CHSE* CH3 .... 30 D6
Meadow Av *MOLD/BUCK* CH7 .... 35 G4
  FLINT CH6 .... 7 J1
Meadowbank *HLYW* CH8 .... 7 H4
Meadow-Bank Cl *FLINT* CH6 * 13 F4
Meadow Cl *CQ* CH5 .... 25 J2
Meadow Crs *WRX/CR/LL* LL12 .... 51 H6
Meadowcroft *CH/BCN* CH1 .... 18 A5
  CHSW/BR CH4 .... 46 E5
Meadow Field Rd
  CHSW/BR CH4 .... 39 G5
Meadow La *CHSE* CH3 .... 40 C5
Meadow Pl *MOLD/BUCK* CH7 .... 43 H4
Meadow Ri *CHSW/BR* CH4 .... 45 J5
Meadow Rd *CHSW/BR* CH4 .... 37 J1
Meadowside *CQ* CH5 .... 35 J1
  MOLD/BUCK CH7 .... 42 E1
Meadowside Ms *CHSW/BR* CH4 ...... 48 A6
Meadows La *CH/BCN* CH1 .... 18 A6
Meadows Pl *CHSW/BR* CH4 * 3 C7
The Meadows *CQ* CH5 .... 25 K3
  FLINT CH6 .... 13 F6
Meadowsway *CHNE* CH2 .... 19 K6
Meadow Vw *CQ* CH5 .... 26 E2
  MOLD/BUCK CH7 .... 45 J1
Mechanics' La *CQ* CH5 .... 26 C4
Medway Cl *CHSW/BR* CH4 .... 39 F5
Meg's La *MOLD/BUCK* CH7 .... 44 E1
Melbourne Rd *CH/BCN* CH1 .... 28 D4
  MOLD/BUCK CH7 .... 42 D4
Melbreck Av *CQ* CH5 .... 35 J1
Melford Pl *CQ* CH5 .... 25 F4
Melin-Y-Dre *HLYW* CH8 .... 11 H2
Melkridge Cl *CHNE* CH2 .... 30 C5

Melrose Av *CHSE* CH3 .... 30 D6
  CQ CH5 .... 25 K4
Melverly Dr *CH/BCN* CH1 .... 28 C4
Melwood Cl *CHSW/BR* CH4 .... 45 J3
Mercer Wy *CHSW/BR* CH4 .... 39 F4
Mercia Dr *MOLD/BUCK* CH7 .... 43 K2
Mercury Ct *CH/BCN* CH1 .... 28 E6
Mercroft *CHSE* CH3 .... 40 C1
Merefield Cl *CQ* CH5 .... 25 F1
Merllyn La *FLINT* CH6 .... 9 H5
Merton Dr *CHSW/BR* CH4 .... 39 G6
Mertyn Downing La *HLYW* CH8 .... 4 A4
Mertyn La *HLYW* CH8 .... 7 G1
The Mews *MOLD/BUCK* CH7 .... 34 E5
Meynell Rd *CH/BCN* CH1 .... 29 G3
Mickelgate *CHSE* CH3 .... 21 G6
Middlecroft *CHSE* CH3 .... 30 A3
Milborne Cl *CHSE* CH3 .... 30 A3
Milford St *MOLD/BUCK* CH7 .... 43 F2
Millais Cl *CQ* CH5 .... 14 E6
Mill Cl *CHNE* CH2 .... 29 K2
Mill Cft *FLINT* CH6 .... 13 J4
Millers Cl *CHSE* CH3 .... 41 J6
Mill La *CHNE* CH2 .... 20 B2
  CQ CH5 .... 25 J2
  MOLD/BUCK CH7 .... 34 D5
Mill St *CHSW/BR* CH4 .... 3 F7
Millview Rd *CQ* CH5 .... 25 J2
Millway *CHSE* CH3 .... 40 A4
Milton Av *CH/BCN* CH1 .... 29 F2
Milton Rd *CH/BCN* CH1 .... 3 F3
Min Awel *FLINT* CH6 .... 13 H5
Minerva Av *CH/BCN* CH1 .... 28 E6
Minfordd Flds
  MOLD/BUCK CH7 .... 42 B5
Moel Fammau Rd
  MOLD/BUCK CH7 .... 33 J6
Moel Ganol *MOLD/BUCK* CH7 .... 42 D5
Moel Gron *MOLD/BUCK* CH7 .... 42 D5
Moel Parc *FLINT* CH6 .... 13 H5
Moel View Rd *MOLD/BUCK* CH7 ... 24 B4
Moel View Rd *MOLD/BUCK* CH7 ... 44 D1
Moelwyn Ct *MOLD/BUCK* CH7 .... 34 A4
Mold Rd *CHSW/BR* CH4 .... 2 B5
  CQ CH5 .... 34 E1
  MOLD/BUCK CH7 .... 47 J3
  MOLD/BUCK CH7 .... 43 J3
  WRX/CR/LL LL12 .... 51 H5
Moldsdale Rd *MOLD/BUCK* CH7 .... 25 G6
Mold Wy *CQ* CH5 .... 25 G6
Mollington Ct *CH/BCN* CH1 .... 18 E5
Monastery Rd *HLYW* CH8 .... 5 F6
Monet Cl *CQ* CH5 .... 14 E6
Montrose Ct *CHSW/BR* CH4 .... 39 F5
Monza Cl *MOLD/BUCK* CH7 .... 34 B6
Moor Av *HLYW* CH8 .... 7 H1
Moor Cft *MOLD/BUCK* CH7 .... 33 K6
Moorcroft Av *CHSE* CH3 .... 40 D1
Moorcroft Crs *CHSE* CH3 .... 30 B6
Moorfields *MOLD/BUCK* CH7 .... 34 E6
Moorfield Ct *CQ* CH5 .... 25 K5
Moorfield Rd *CQ* CH5 .... 25 K5
Moorhouse Cl *CHNE* CH2 .... 29 K3
Moor La *CHSE* CH3 .... 41 J5
  CHSE CH3 .... 47 C6
  CQ CH5 .... 36 C2
  FLINT CH6 .... 7 H1
Morgan Cl *CH/BCN* CH1 .... 29 E5
Morley Av *CQ* CH5 .... 25 K4
Morley Cl *CHNE* CH2 .... 21 H6
Mornington Crs
  MOLD/BUCK CH7 .... 35 G5
Mortlake Crs *CHSE* CH3 .... 40 C1
Morton Rd *CH/BCN* CH1 .... 28 E4
Moss Bank *CH/BCN* CH1 .... 29 J4
Moss Gv *CHSW/BR* CH4 .... 38 D4
Mossley Ct *CQ* CH5 .... 36 A2
Moston Rd *CHNE* CH2 .... 19 J5
Mostyn Pl *CH/BCN* CH1 .... 28 D5
Mostyn St *CQ* CH5 .... 25 J2
Mountain Cl *WRX/CR/LL* LL12 .... 51 J4
Mountain Vw *CHSW/BR* CH4 .... 38 E4
  WRX/CR/LL LL12 .... 51 J4
Mountain View Av
  MOLD/BUCK CH7 .... 34 A5
Mountain View Cl *CQ* CH5 * 25 J5
Mount Cl *MOLD/BUCK* CH7 .... 43 K3
Mountfield Rd *CQ* CH5 .... 25 K5
Mount Pl *CHSE* CH3 .... 3 J3
Mount Pleasant
  MOLD/BUCK CH7 .... 48 A5
Mount Pleasant Av *FLINT* CH6 .... 13 G4
Mount Pleasant Rd
  MOLD/BUCK CH7 .... 34 E6
Mount Pleasant *CHSW/BR* CH4 ...... 39 F3
Mount Tabor Cl *CHSW/BR* CH4 .... 45 J5
The Mount *CHSE* CH3 .... 3 K4
  HLYW CH8 .... 8 B5
Mount Wy *CHSE* CH3 .... 41 J6
Muirfield Rd *MOLD/BUCK* CH7 ...... 34 C5
Mulberry Av *CHNE* CH2 .... 28 E5
Music Hall Pas *CH/BCN* CH1 * 2 D4
Myrica Gv *CHNE* CH2 .... 30 D5
Myrtle Av *CHSW/BR* CH4 .... 46 E5
Myrtle Cv *CHNE* CH2 .... 30 C5
Myrtle La *HLYW* CH8 .... 8 B3
Myrtle Rd *MOLD/BUCK* CH7 .... 34 B5

N

Nant Derw *MOLD/BUCK* CH7 .... 42 D3
Nant Eos *HLYW* CH8 .... 7 H5
Nant Garmon *MOLD/BUCK* CH7 .... 42 E3
Nant Glyn *MOLD/BUCK* CH7 .... 42 E4
Nant Mawr Crs
  MOLD/BUCK CH7 .... 34 C6
Nant Rd *CQ* CH5 .... 15 F6
  HLYW CH8 .... 12 A3
Nant y Coed *HLYW* CH8 .... 8 B2
Nant-y-Gaer *MOLD/BUCK* CH7 ...... 42 E4
Nant-y-Glyn *FLINT* CH6 .... 9 G4
Naomi Cl *CH/BCN* CH1 .... 28 D3
Napier Rd *CHNE* CH2 .... 19 J6
Narrow La *HLYW* CH8 .... 7 H5

Nefyn Cl *CQ* CH5 .... 24 E1
Nelson St *CH/BCN* CH1 .... 3 G2
  CQ CH5 .... 25 K2
Neston Dr *CHNE* CH2 .... 29 K3
Neston Vw *FLINT* CH6 .... 9 H5
Neville Dr *CHSE* CH3 .... 40 D1
Neville Rd *CHSE* CH3 .... 40 D1
Nevin Rd *MOLD/BUCK* CH7 .... 28 E6
Newbridge Rd
  MOLD/BUCK CH7 .... 33 H4
Newbury Rd *CHSW/BR* CH4 .... 39 F4
Newby Wk *CQ* CH5 .... 14 E6
New Crane Bank *CH/BCN* CH1 .... 2 B4
New Crane St *CH/BCN* CH1 .... 2 B3
Newcroft *CH/BCN* CH1 .... 18 A4
Newgate Rw *CH/BCN* CH1 * 2 E4
Newgate St *CH/BCN* CH1 * 2 E4
Newhall Ct *CHNE* CH2 .... 30 A2
New Hall Ct *CHSW/BR* CH4 .... 39 F4
Newhall Rd *CHNE* CH2 .... 30 A2
New Park Rd *CQ* CH5 .... 25 J4
New Rd *CQ* CH5 .... 25 H5
  HLYW CH8 .... 7 K2
New Roskell Sq *FLINT* CH6 .... 13 H2
Newry Ct *CHNE* CH2 .... 29 K4
Newry Rd *CHNE* CH2 .... 29 K4
Newry Pk East *CHNE* CH2 .... 29 K4
Newry Pk *CHNE* CH2 .... 25 H1
  MOLD/BUCK CH7 .... 25 H1
Newthorn Pl *MOLD/BUCK* CH7 ...... 24 B4
Newton Av *MOLD/BUCK* CH7 .... 24 B4
Newton Dr *MOLD/BUCK* CH7 .... 30 B3
Newton Hall Ct *CHNE* CH2 .... 30 B3
Newton Hall Dr *CHNE* CH2 .... 30 B3
Newton La *CHNE* CH2 .... 30 A3
Newton Park Vw *CHNE* CH2 .... 30 B3
Newtown Cl *CH/BCN* CH1 .... 3 F2
New Union St *CQ* CH5 .... 15 F6
Nicholas Ct *CH/BCN* CH1 .... 2 C5
Nicholas St *CH/BCN* CH1 .... 2 C4
Nicholas Street Ms *CH/BCN* CH1 ..... 2 C5
Nick Olson Cl *CHNE* CH2 .... 21 H6
Nield Ct *CHNE* CH2 .... 29 K1
The Nook *CHNE* CH2 .... 30 A4
  CHSE CH3 .... 40 A4
  CHSW/BR CH4 .... 38 E4
  CQ CH5 .... 26 B6
Norfolk Rd *CHSE* CH3 .... 30 B3
Norley Dr *CHSE* CH3 .... 40 E1
Normanby Dr *CQ* CH5 .... 25 F2
Normandy Rd *CHNE* CH2 .... 19 J5
Norman St *CQ* CH5 .... 25 K4
Norman Wy *CH/BCN* CH1 .... 28 E3
Norris Rd *CQ* CH5 .... 35 J2
Northern Pathway
  CHSW/BR CH4 .... 3 G7
Northgate Av *CHNE* CH2 .... 29 E1
Northgate St *CH/BCN* CH1 .... 2 C5
North Gn *CQ* CH5 .... 26 E2
Northop Cl *CQ* CH5 .... 25 J4
Northop Rd *FLINT* CH6 .... 23 G3
  MOLD/BUCK CH7 .... 33 G2
Northop Rd (Ffordd
  Llaneurgain) *FLINT* CH6 .... 13 G6
North Rd *CQ* CH5 .... 15 H4
  HLYW CH8 .... 7 K2
North St *CHSE* CH3 .... 40 C1
  CHSW/BR CH4 .... 38 E3
  CQ CH5 .... 25 K3
Northway *CHSW/BR* CH4 .... 39 G3
Norton Av *CHSW/BR* CH4 .... 38 D4
Norton Rd *CHSE* CH3 .... 30 C5
Norwood Dr *CHSW/BR* CH4 .... 39 H5
Nun's Rd *CH/BCN* CH1 .... 2 C5
The Nurseries *FLINT* CH6 .... 13 F4

O

Oak Bank La *CHNE* CH2 .... 30 E1
Oak Cl *CQ* CH5 .... 26 D1
Oakdale Cl *CHSW/BR* CH4 .... 47 F1
Oak Dr *CHSW/BR* CH4 .... 46 E5
  MOLD/BUCK CH7 .... 34 D4
  MOLD/BUCK CH7 .... 50 A1
Oakenholt La *FLINT* CH6 .... 14 B4
Oakfield Av *CHNE* CH2 .... 20 A6
Oakfield Dr *CHNE* CH2 .... 20 A6
Oakfield Rd *CH/BCN* CH1 .... 28 C4
  CQ CH5 .... 35 J1
  CHSE CH3 .... 34 E6
Oak Gv *MOLD/BUCK* CH7 .... 38 D5
  FLINT CH6 .... 13 J6
Oaklands *CHSE* CH3 .... 31 G3
Oaklea Av *CHSW/BR* CH4 .... 30 B4
Oakley Cl *CHSE* CH3 .... 26 C6
Oakmere Dr *CHSE* CH3 .... 40 D2
Oak Pk *MOLD/BUCK* CH7 .... 34 D4
Oak Rd *MOLD/BUCK* CH7 .... 39 F4
The Oaks *CHSW/BR* CH4 .... 39 H5
The Oaks Dr *CHNE* CH2 .... 29 J1
Oak St *MOLD/BUCK* CH7 .... 43 F1
Oak Tree Cl *CQ* CH5 .... 25 H3
Oak Tree Ct *CQ* CH5 .... 34 E5
Oaktree Ct *CHNE* CH2 .... 30 C5
Oakwood Cl *MOLD/BUCK* CH7 .... 42 E1
Oakwood Vis *CQ* CH5 .... 25 J5
Oak Aston Mt *CQ* CH5 .... 25 H5
Old Bank La *MOLD/BUCK* CH7 .... 44 D1
Old Chester Rd *CQ* CH5 .... 25 H6
  CHNE CH2 .... 8 A4
Oldfield Crs *CHSW/BR* CH4 .... 39 H5
Oldfield Dr *CHSE* CH3 .... 30 E6
Old Hall Gdns *CHNE* CH2 .... 30 B3
Old Hall Pk *CHSE* CH3 .... 31 H3
Old Hall Pl *CH/BCN* CH1 * 2 C6
Old Hall Rd *CQ* CH5 .... 35 J1
Old Liverpool Rd *CQ* CH5 .... 35 G1
Old London Rd *FLINT* CH6 .... 12 C2
Old Mold Rd *CQ* CH5 .... 35 G6
The Old Orch *CQ* CH5 .... 35 G2
Old Paper Mill La *FLINT* CH6 .... 14 A3
Old Port Sq *CH/BCN* CH1 .... 28 D5
Old Seals Wy *CH/BCN* CH1 .... 29 G5
Old Wrexham Rd
  MOLD/BUCK CH7 .... 39 J3
Onslow Rd *CH/BCN* CH1 .... 28 D4

Orchard Cl *CHNE* CH2 .... 29 J1
  CQ CH5 .... 26 E1
  MOLD/BUCK CH7 .... 34 D4
Orchard Ct *CHSE* CH3 .... 40 D2
Orchard Cft *CHSE* CH3 .... 30 C6
The Orchards *CQ* CH5 .... 31 E1
Orchard Cl *MOLD/BUCK* CH7 .... 2 E5
The Orchard *CHSE* CH3 .... 40 C1
Orchard Wy *MOLD/BUCK* CH7 .... 42 E3
Orchil Cl *CHSE* CH3 .... 40 A4
Ormonde Rd *CHNE* CH2 .... 3 G2
Ormonde St *CH/BCN* CH1 * 3 G2
Osbourne Ct *CQ* CH5 .... 15 F5
Oulton Av *CHNE* CH2 .... 30 A2
Oulton Pl *CH/BCN* CH1 .... 29 G3
Overdale Av *MOLD/BUCK* CH7 .... 26 A3
Overlea Crs *CQ* CH5 .... 26 A3
Overlea Dr *CQ* CH5 .... 26 A3
Overleigh Ct *CHSW/BR* CH4 .... 38 E6
Overleigh Rd *CHSW/BR* CH4 .... 39 F6
Overleigh Rd *MOLD/BUCK* CH7 ..... 42 A3
Overleigh Ter *CHSW/BR* CH4 * 39 F6
Overton Cl *MOLD/BUCK* CH7 .... 34 B6
Overwood La *CH/BCN* CH1 .... 18 D6
Overwood La *CH/BCN* CH1 .... 28 D5
Owen Cl *CHSW/BR* CH4 .... 28 B1
Oxford Rd *CHSW/BR* CH4 .... 39 F4

P

Padarn Cl *CHSW/BR* CH4 .... 38 A6
Paddock Rw *CH/BCN* CH1 * 2 E4
The Paddocks *CH/BCN* CH1 .... 18 C1
The Paddock *CHSW/BR* CH4 .... 39 G4
  CQ CH5 .... 26 E1
Paddock Wy *MOLD/BUCK* CH7 .... 46 A6
  MOLD/BUCK CH7 .... 42 E1
Padeswood Ct
  MOLD/BUCK CH7 .... 34 D5
Padeswood Dr
  MOLD/BUCK CH7 .... 34 D5
Padeswood Rd North
  MOLD/BUCK CH7 .... 34 D5
Padeswood Rd South
  MOLD/BUCK CH7 .... 44 D1
Palace Cl *FLINT* CH6 .... 12 C2
Palatine Cl *CHSE* CH3 .... 31 H3
Palgrave Cl *CH/BCN* CH1 .... 29 G3
Palmerston Crs *CQ* CH5 .... 35 J2
Palmerstone Cl *CH/BCN* CH1 .... 29 G3
Pant Glas *MOLD/BUCK* CH7 .... 33 H4
Pant Isa *MOLD/BUCK* CH7 .... 33 G2
Panton Rd *CHNE* CH2 .... 30 A2
Pant Ucha *MOLD/BUCK* CH7 .... 33 G2
Pant y Fownog Dr
  CHSW/BR CH4 .... 3 G7
Paper Mill La *FLINT* CH6 .... 14 A3
The Parade *CH/BCN* CH1 .... 28 B1
Paradise *CHSW/BR* CH4 .... 3 G5
Parc Bryn Castell *CQ* CH5 .... 35 J1
Parc Capel *HLYW* CH8 .... 11 H3
Parc Gorsedd *HLYW* CH8 * 6 B1
Parc Hendy *MOLD/BUCK* CH7 .... 42 D5
Parc Issa *MOLD/BUCK* CH7 .... 34 A4
Park Av *CH/BCN* CH1 .... 29 J4
  CHSW/BR CH4 .... 38 A6
  CQ CH5 .... 46 E1
  FLINT CH6 .... 13 J6
  HLYW CH8 .... 8 B1
Park Crs *CHSW/BR* CH4 .... 45 J5
  HLYW CH8 .... 7 K2
Park Dr *CHSE* CH3 .... 30 E6
Park Dr South *CHNE* CH2 .... 30 A4
Parkfield Rd *CHSW/BR* CH4 .... 47 G1
Parkgate Rd *CH/BCN* CH1 .... 18 C1
Park Gv *CQ* CH5 .... 15 F6
Park Hall Rd *HLYW* CH8 .... 5 F6
Parkhouse Ms
  MOLD/BUCK CH7 * 43 F1
Park House Ms
  MOLD/BUCK CH7 * 43 F1
Park La *CHSW/BR* CH4 .... 45 J5
  HLYW CH8 .... 8 B1
Park Rd *FLINT* CH6 .... 13 J6
  MOLD/BUCK CH7 .... 34 E6
Park Rd West *CHSW/BR* CH4 .... 38 D6
Parkside *MOLD/BUCK* CH7 .... 34 D4
Parkside Av (Rhodfa
  Ger y Parc) *CQ* CH5 * 24 E5
The Parks *CHNE* CH2 .... 30 A4
Park St *CH/BCN* CH1 .... 2 E5
The Park *CHSE* CH3 .... 31 G3
  CQ CH5 .... 24 E5
Park Vw *MOLD/BUCK* CH7 .... 34 D4
Park Wk *CHNE* CH2 .... 29 J4
Park Wy *CH/BCN* CH1 .... 18 C1
Parkway *CQ* CH5 .... 16 A6
Parrs Cl *CQ* CH5 .... 42 E1
Patten Cl *CQ* CH5 .... 35 J2
Peach Fld *CHSE* CH3 .... 40 D2
Pearl La *CHSE* CH3 .... 40 C1
Pear Tree Cl *CQ* CH5 .... 26 D1
Pear Tree Wy *CHNE* CH2 .... 30 D2
Peckforton Wy *CHNE* CH2 .... 30 A4
Peel Ter *CH/BCN* CH1 * 3 H2
Pemba Dr *MOLD/BUCK* CH7 .... 34 A6
Pemberton Rd *CH/BCN* CH1 .... 28 C3
Pembroke Cl *CHSW/BR* CH4 .... 39 F4
  CQ CH5 .... 25 J4
Pembry Ri *CQ* CH5 .... 25 K3
Penfold Hey *CHNE* CH2 .... 30 A4
Penfold Wy *CHSW/BR* CH4 .... 38 A6
Pengwialys Av *CQ* CH5 .... 25 F1
Penian Dr *CQ* CH5 .... 25 J4
Pen Lan La *HLYW* CH8 * 7 G1
Penley Rd *MOLD/BUCK* CH7 .... 34 B6
Pen Lon *FLINT* CH6 .... 8 E4
Penmon Cl *CH/BCN* CH1 .... 28 C4

nant St CH5 .... 25 H1
nny Bank Cl CHSW/BR CH4 ..... 46 D1
nrho HLYW CH8 .... 4 B2
nrhos Ct CQ CH5 .... 24 E4
nrhyn HLYW CH8 .... 8 C2
nslv Av CHNE CH2 .... 29 K5
ntland Cl CHSE CH3 .... 30 D6
ntre La MOLD/BUCK CH7 .... 34 C3
ntre Rd HLYW CH8 .... 11 J5
n-y-Ball Hi HLYW CH8 .... 7 J3
n-y-Ball St HLYW CH8 .... 7 K3
n-y-Bryn FLINT CH6 .... 13 H6
   MOLD/BUCK CH7 .... 42 E3
   WRX/GR/LL LL12 .... 51 J4
n-y-Coed Rd
   MOLD/BUCK CH7 .... 35 G4
n-y-Garreg Cl
n-y-Glyn FLINT CH6 .... 34 A5
n y Lan CQ CH5 .... 9 G4
n y Lon MOLD/BUCK CH7 .... 43 J3
n y Maes Gdns HLYW CH8 .... 8 B3
   CHSW/BR CH4 .... 34 C6
nymaes MOLD/BUCK CH7
n-y-Maes Gdns HLYW CH8 .... 8 B3
n-y-Maes Rd (Fford
   Pen-y-Maes) HLYW CH8 ...... 8 D2
nymynvdd Rd
   CHSW/BR CH4 .... 45 J3
n-y-Pentre
   CHSW/BR CH7 .... 33 H4
pper St CH7 .... 2 E5
   CHSE CH3 .... 41 F2
rcival Ct CHNE CH2 .... 19 J6
rcival Rd CHSW/BR CH4 .... 19 J6
rcy Rd CHSW/BR CH4 .... 39 K3
renna Ct FLINT CH6 .... 14 D4
lip St CQ CH5 .... 26 E6
llips Rd CH/BCN CH1 .... 28 D5
llip St CHNE CH2 .... 3 H1
oenix St CQ CH5 .... 25 J1
kering St CHNE CH2 .... 3 H1
kmere Dr CHSE CH3 .... 40 D2
ton Gorse La CHNE CH2 .... 20 D6
ton La CHNE CH2 .... 20 E1
rce St CQ CH5 .... 25 J1
rxpoint Ct CH/BCN CH1 .... 2 D5
eon House La
   WRX/GR/LL LL12 .... 51 H4
e Crest FLINT CH6 .... 12 B4
e Gdns CHNE CH2 .... 29 J2
e Gv CHNE CH2 .... 30 D4
   MOLD/BUCK CH7 .... 34 A6
e Pines CQ CH5 .... 25 H5
e Tree Cl CHSW/BR CH4 .... 35 H5
ewood Av CQ CH5 .... 25 C1
ewood Rd
   MOLD/BUCK CH7 .... 35 H5
fold Cft CHSW/BR CH4 .... 33 K4
fold La CHSW/BR CH4 .... 39 K4
got Cft CHSE CH3 .... 40 D3
ers Ct CHNE CH2 .... 30 D4
ers Cl CHNE CH2 .... 21 H6
pins Ct CQ CH5 .... 25 J3
rgil HLYW CH8 .... 8 B5
mans La CQ CH5 .... 36 A1
s Newton La CHNE CH2 .... 30 B4
s-yn-Rhos CHSW/BR CH4 ...... 45 H5
et La CHSW/BR CH4 .... 51 H1
asant Vw CHSW/BR CH4 .... 45 K3
mstall Ct CHNE CH2 .... 21 H6
mstall La CHNE CH2 .... 21 H5
mstall Wy CHNE CH2 .... 21 H5
ugh La CHSE CH3 .... 41 H3
m CQ CH5 .... 2 E3
miey Cl CHSE CH3 .... 40 E1
m Ter CH/BCN CH1 .... 2 C2
mouth St CQ CH5 .... 25 J2
tybodkin Hi
   MOLD/BUCK CH7 .... 50 B3
lar Av CQ CH5 .... 25 E5
lar Cl CQ CH5 .... 25 G2
lar Cl CQ CH5 .... 25 G6
lar Rd CHSW/BR CH4 .... 39 F5
e Poplars CQ CH5 .... 35 H3
lop Field Dr CHSW/BR CH4 ... 45 J4
ch La WRX/GR/LL LL12 .... 51 H6
ters Cft CHSE CH3 .... 31 H5
st Office La HLYW CH8 .... 7 F3
ters Wl MOLD/BUCK CH7 ...... 34 C5
well Rd MOLD/BUCK CH7 ...... 44 C1
well's Orch CHSW/BR CH4 .... 39 J5
wey La CH/BCN CH1 .... 18 B1
wys Cl CQ CH5 .... 26 B4
   MOLD/BUCK CH7 .... 34 E4
wys Ct CH/BCN CH1 .... 2 C3
   Precinct Wy
n Av MOLD/BUCK CH7 .... 34 A6
nton Pl CHSW/BR CH4 .... 39 K3
scot St CHNE CH2 .... 3 J1
toria St CHSW/BR CH4 .... 39 K3
nrose Cl CHSE CH3 .... 40 D4
nrose St CQ CH5 .... 25 G1
ce of Wales Av FLINT CH6 .... 13 G3
ce W... HLYW CH8 .... 8 B2
nces Av CH/BCN CH1 .... 3 H5
nces Dr FLINT CH6
nces Av MOLD/BUCK CH7 ..... 34 D6
ncess St CHNE CH2 .... 2 C4
ncess St CQ CH5 .... 25 G1
nce's St CQ CH5 .... 2 C1
nce William Av CH/BCN CH1 .. 13 H5
nce William Rd CQ CH5 .... 35 J1
nce William Gdns CQ CH5 .... 26 C6
ors Cl CQ CH5 .... 25 J4
ory Cl CH/BCN CH1 .... 29 J4
ory La CH/BCN CH1 .... 3 F4
rate Wk CHSE CH3 .... 40 D5
mised Land La CHSE CH3 .... 41 G5
spect Ct CQ CH5 .... 25 J6
sser Rd CHNE CH2 .... 19 H5
nan Wy CQ CH5 .... 28 D3
ord Av CHSW/BR CH4 .... 48 A6
ord Rd CHNE CH2 .... 28 E3
l Glas MOLD/BUCK CH7 .... 42 E2

Pwll y Hwyaden FLINT CH6 .... 13 H6
Pyecroft St CHSW/BR CH4 ..... 39 K3

Q

Quarry Cl MOLD/BUCK CH7 .... 24 B4
Quarry La CHSW/BR CH4 .... 41 F3
   CHSE CH3 .... 25 G2
   MOLD/BUCK CH7 * 33 G4
Quay La CQ CH5 .... 15 G6
Queen's Av CH/BCN CH1 .... 3 H3
   CO CH5 .... 2 E5
   CO CH5 .... 26 E5
Queens Av FLINT CH6 .... 13 H4
Queensbury Dr FLINT CH6 .... 12 E3
Queens Crs CHSW/BR CH4 ... 30 A1
Queens Dr CHSW/BR CH4 ...... 3 H6
Queens Dr MOLD/BUCK CH7 . 34 D6
Queen's La MOLD/BUCK CH7 . 43 G4
Queen's Park Rd CHSW/BR CH4 3 F7
Queen's Rd CH/BCN CH1 .... 3 F3
Queen's Rd CHSW/BR CH4 ..... 3 H2
Queen's Rd CHSE CH3 .... 30 D6
Queen's Rd CQ CH5 .... 25 J1
   HLYW CH8 .... 5 G5
Queen St CH/BCN CH1 .... 2 E5
   CHSE CH3 .... 26 B3
   FLINT CH6 .... 13 H3
   MOLD/BUCK CH7 .... 2 B3
Queen's Wy CHSW/BR CH4 ... 37 F6
Queensway CO CH5 .... 25 J2
   WRX/GR/LL LL12 .... 51 K6

R

Radford Cl CQ CH5 .... 25 J1
Radnor Cl CQ CH5 .... 26 B4
Radnor Dr CHSW/BR CH4 ...... 39 G5
Raewood Av CQ CH5 .... 35 H2
Raikes La MOLD/BUCK CH7 * . 33 F3
Rake La CHSE CH3 .... 41 J2
   CHSW/BR CH4 .... 49 C4
Rake Wy CHSW/BR CH4 .... 18 A5
Ramsden Ct CHSW/BR CH4 ... 39 F6
Ramwoath Ct CHNE CH2 .... 21 K4
Rawson Rd CH/BCN CH1 .... 28 E5
Raymond St CH/BCN CH1 .... 2 C3
Rayon Rd HLYW CH8 .... 8 C1
Rectors La CQ CH5 .... 25 G2
Rectory Cft CHSE CH3 .... 13 G4
Rectory La CQ CH5 .... 36 B2
Red Hall Av CQ CH5 .... 25 H1
Redhill Wy CHSW/BR CH4 ...... 39 F4
Redland Ct CHSW/BR CH4 ..... 33 H5
Red Rd MOLD/BUCK CH7 ...... 34 D4
Redwood Cl CHSW/BR CH4 .... 33 H5
Reece La CHNE CH2 .... 21 G6
Reeves Rd CHSE CH3 .... 40 D2
Regency Ct CHNE CH2 .... 21 G6
Regents Cl CHSE CH3 .... 30 D6
Reservoir Ter CHSE CH3 .... 3 K3
Reynolds Rd FLINT CH6 .... 9 K6
Rhodfa Cilcain
   MOLD/BUCK CH7 .... 42 E4
Rhodfa Eurgain
   (Eurgain Av) CQ CH5 .... 24 E2
Rhodfa Ger y Parc
   (Parkside Av) CQ CH5 .... 24 E2
Rhodfa Mynydd
   MOLD/BUCK CH7 .... 42 E4
Rhos Av CHSW/BR CH4 .... 45 H5
Rhos Estyn La WRX/GR/LL LL12 51 J5
Rhoslan HLYW CH8 .... 8 A2
Rhos Rd CHSW/BR CH4 .... 45 H5
Rhoswen FLINT CH6 .... 13 H5
Rhuddlan Ct CHSW/BR CH4 ... 39 F4
Rhuddlan Rd CH/BCN CH1 ..... 28 D4
   MOLD/BUCK CH7 .... 34 E3
Rhyd Osber MOLD/BUCK CH7 50 A4
Richards Cft CHSE CH3 .... 40 C3
Richmond Ct CHNE CH2 .... 3 K3
Richmond Crs CHSE CH3 .... 40 C1
Richmond Rd CQ CH5 .... 25 H2
Ridgehill Dr FLINT CH6 .... 9 G4
Ridgeway Cl CQ CH5 .... 25 F2
The Ridgeway CQ CH5 .... 25 K6
   HLYW CH8 .... 8 B5
   MOLD/BUCK CH7 .... 34 B4
The Ridings CH/BCN CH1 .... 40 E1
Ring Rd CHSE CH3 .... 18 A5
Ringway CHSE CH3 .... 41 K5
Riverbank FLINT CH6 .... 8 D2
River La CHSW/BR CH4 .... 39 F4
River Rd CQ CH5 .... 15 H5
Riverside Ct MOLD/BUCK CH7 34 C4
Riverside Pk CQ CH5 .... 26 D2
Riversmead CQ CH5 .... 40 C5
River Vw CQ CH5 .... 15 F6
Robinsons Cft CHSE CH3 ...... 40 D3
Rock La WRX/GR/LL LL12 ..... 51 G6
Rockliffe La FLINT CH6 .... 14 B3
Rock Rd CQ CH5 .... 15 G6
Roebourne Ri CH/BCN CH1 ... 28 D2
Roman Dr CH/BCN CH1 .... 28 D2
Romans Wy FLINT CH6 .... 9 J6
Roman Wy MOLD/BUCK CH7 . 34 D6
The Rookery FLINT CH6 .... 47 F1
Rose Cl CH/BCN CH1 .... 28 D2
Rosedene Cl CHNE CH2 .... 20 A6
Rosehill HLYW CH8 .... 8 A4
Rose La MOLD/BUCK CH7 .... 34 A6
Rosemary Cl CHSW/BR CH4 .. 47 C1
Rosewood Av CHNE CH2 .... 29 K5
Rosewood Gv CHSW/BR CH4 18 B6
   MOLD/BUCK CH7 .... 50 A4
Rosslyn Cl CQ CH5 .... 26 E6
Rosslyn Rd CHSE CH3 .... 30 D5

Rothesay Rd CHSW/BR CH4 .. 39 G3
Roughlyn Crs CHSW/BR CH4 . 48 D3
Round Hill Meadow CHSE CH3 40 D5
Rowan Cl MOLD/BUCK CH7 ... 35 H6
Rowan Ct CHNE CH2 .... 14 E5
Rowan Pk CHSE CH3 .... 41 F3
Rowan Pl CHNE CH2 .... 30 D4
Rowan Rd CQ CH5 .... 25 J5
The Rowans CHSW/BR CH4 ... 47 F1
Rowcliffe Av CHSW/BR CH4 ... 55 H6
Rowden Crs CQ CH5 .... 25 J2
Rowden St CQ CH5 .... 25 J2
Rowley's Dr CQ CH5 .... 26 A2
Rowton Bridge Rd CHSE CH3 41 G3
Rowton La CHSE CH3 .... 41 G5
Royal Dr FLINT CH6 .... 12 E3
Rue St Gregoire HLYW CH8 ..... 7 F4
Rufus Court Rw CH/BCN CH1 .. 2 D5
Rumney Cl CQ CH5 .... 24 E4
Rushfield Rd CHSW/BR CH4 ... 39 H5
Sevenacre Ct FLINT CH6 .... 8 J5
Russell St CHNE CH2 .... 3 G3
Ruthin Cl MOLD/BUCK CH7 ... 34 C6
Ruthin Rd MOLD/BUCK CH7 ... 42 D4
Rutland Ct CQ CH5 .... 25 K4
Rutland Pl CHNE CH2 .... 30 C3
Rydal Dr MOLD/BUCK CH7 .... 34 E4
Rydal Gv CHSW/BR CH4 .... 25 J1
Ryeland St CQ CH5

S

Saddlery Wy CH/BCN CH1 .... 2 B5
St Andrew's Dr
   MOLD/BUCK CH7 .... 34 C5
St Annes Ct CHSE CH3 .... 2 E2
St Anne St CH/BCN CH1 .... 2 E2
St Asaph Rd HLYW CH8 .... 8 A3
St Bartholomews Ct CQ CH5 .. 27 J2
St Catherine's Cl FLINT CH6 .. 13 G3
St Chad's Rd CH/BCN CH1 .... 29 F4
St Christophers Cl CHNE CH2 19 J6
St Cynfarch's Av
   WRX/GR/LL LL12 .... 51 J5
St David's Cl CQ CH5 .... 26 B4
St Davids Cl FLINT CH6 .... 13 H5
   HLYW CH8 .... 8 A3
St David's Cl FLINT CH6 .... 13 H5
St David's Ct CQ CH5 .... 25 J1
St David's Dr CQ CH5 .... 25 C1
St David's La MOLD/BUCK CH7 43 G2
St David's Ter CHSW/BR CH4 . 38 C3
St Ethelwolds St CQ CH5 .... 25 K4
St Georges CH/BCN CH1 .... 2 E5
St George's Crs CHSE CH3 .... 41 J5
   CHSW/BR CH4 .... 3 G7
St Ives Wy CQ CH5 .... 26 E5
St James Av CHNE CH2 .... 30 D2
St James St CH/BCN CH1 .... 3 F2
St Johns Cl CHSW/BR CH4 .... 45 K3
St John's Cl MOLD/BUCK CH7 34 D5
St John's Rear Rd
   CHSW/BR CH4 .... 3 G7
St John's Rd CHSW/BR CH4 ... 3 G6
St John St CHNE CH2 .... 2 E4
St Mark's Av CQ CH5 .... 25 F1
St Marks Rd CHSW/BR CH4 ... 39 H6
St Martin's Wy CH/BCN CH1 .... 2 C3
St Mary's Cl MOLD/BUCK CH7 24 B4
St Mary's Dr MOLD/BUCK CH7 34 B4
St Mary's Ms MOLD/BUCK CH7 2 E6
St Mary's Rd CHSW/BR CH4 .. 48 A5
St Mary's Wy CHSW/BR CH4 .. 37 G5
St Mellor's Rd MOLD/BUCK CH7 34 C5
St Michaels Rw CH/BCN CH1 * . 2 E5
St Michaels St CH/BCN CH1 .... 2 E5
St Olave St CH/BCN CH1 .... 2 E6
St Oswalds CH/BCN CH1 .... 2 E2
St Oswalds Wy CH/BCN CH1 ... 3 F3
St Peter's Pk MOLD/BUCK CH7 23 G5
St Peters Wy CHNE CH2 .... 21 H6
St Thomas Pathway
   CHNE CH2 .... 14 E4
St Thomas's Ct HLYW CH8 ..... 23 G2
St Werburgh St CH/BCN CH1 ... 2 E4
Saith-Aelwyd Pk HLYW CH8 ..... 7 G1
Salerno Rd CHNE CH2 .... 19 H5
Salisbury Av CHNE CH2 .... 38 D4
Salisbury St CH/BCN CH1 ...... 29 H5
   CQ CH5 .... 25 K2
Salmon Leap CHSW/BR CH4 ... 3 F6
Salter's La CHNE CH2 .... 20 E6
Saltney Ferry Rd
   CHSW/BR CH4 .... 38 B3
Salusbury St FLINT CH6 .... 13 H2
Samuel St CQ CH5 .... 3 G2
Sandiieigh CHNE CH2 .... 30 A4
Sandon Rd CHNE CH2 .... 29 K4
Sandown Rd CQ CH5 .... 25 J4
Sandown Ter CHSE CH3 .... 3 K4
Sandpiper Cl CHSW/BR CH4 .. 49 H2
Sandringham Av CHSE CH3 ... 30 C6
Sandrock Rd CHSE CH3 .... 30 C6
Sandwood Av CHSW/BR CH4 . 47 F1
Sandy Cl CHSE CH3 .... 40 E5
   MOLD/BUCK CH7 .... 42 E4
Sandy La CHSE CH3 .... 40 C2
   CHSW/BR CH4 .... 46 E6
   CHSW/BR CH4 .... 38 E5
   CQ CH5 .... 25 J5
   FLINT CH6 .... 9 F4
Sandy Wy CQ CH5 .... 24 E2
Sarn La WRX/GR/LL LL12 ...... 51 J6
Saughall Hey CHSW/BR CH4 .. 18 A5
Saughall Rd CH/BCN CH1 ...... 28 E2
Saxon Wy CH/BCN CH1 .... 28 E2
School La CHNE CH2 .... 21 G6
   CHSE CH3 .... 41 H3
   FLINT CH6 .... 23 G2
   MOLD/BUCK CH7 .... 50 A4
School St CHNE CH2 .... 30 A5
Scots Rd CQ CH5 .... 15 H6
Seahill Rd CHSW/BR CH4 ...... 17 K6
Sealand Av CQ CH5 .... 26 D1

   HLYW CH8 .... 8 B3
Sealand Rd CH/BCN CH1 .... 2 A2
   CH/BCN CH1 .... 28 A3
Seathwaite Wy CQ CH5 .... 24 E2
Seaville St CQ CH5 .... 3 H3
Sebring Av MOLD/BUCK CH7 . 24 D4
Second Av CQ CH5 .... 16 D3
   FLINT CH6 .... 15 G4
Sedgefield Rd CH/BCN CH1 ... 28 D4
Sedum Cl FLINT CH6 .... 40 C4
Sefton Rd CHNE CH2 .... 30 D2
Selkirk Dr CHSW/BR CH4 ...... 39 G5
Selkirk Rd CHSW/BR CH4 ...... 39 G5
Seller St CH/BCN CH1 .... 3 F3
Selsdon Cl MOLD/BUCK CH7 . 34 C5
Selsdon Ct CHSW/BR CH4 ..... 38 E5
Sens Cl CQ CH5 .... 35 K6
Serenity La CQ CH5 .... 35 K6
The Serpentine CHSW/BR CH4 39 H5
Shaftesbury Av CHSE CH3 ..... 30 B5
Shaftesbury Dr FLINT CH6 ..... 12 E3
Shakespeare Av CQ CH5 .... 25 J3
Shannon Cl CHSW/BR CH4 .... 38 E5
Shavington Av CHNE CH2 ...... 30 B5
Shaw Cl CQ CH5 .... 35 G2
Shed La CHSE CH3 .... 30 C6
Sheldon Av CHNE CH2 .... 30 C6
Shelley Cl CQ CH5 .... 35 G2
Shelley Rd CH/BCN CH1 .... 29 F2
Shepherd's La CHNE CH2 ...... 29 K3
Sheraton Rd CHSE CH3 .... 41 K5
Sherbourne Av CHSW/BR CH4 39 H5
Sheridan Av CQ CH5 .... 35 G2
Sheringham Cl CHSW/BR CH4 38 E5
Sherwood Rd CHNE CH2 .... 28 E3
Shipbrook Rd CHSE CH3 .... 30 B2
Shipgate St CH/BCN CH1 .... 2 E6
Shire Vw MOLD/BUCK CH7 .... 43 F2
Shocklach Rd CHNE CH2 .... 30 A2
Shotton Ct CQ CH5 .... 16 C2
Shot Tower Cl CH/BCN CH1 ..... 3 H3
Shotwick La FLINT CH6 .... 27 H5
Shotwick Rd CQ CH5 .... 16 C2
Shrewsbury Wy CHSW/BR CH4 39 F4
Sibell St CH/BCN CH1 .... 3 G1
Siddeley Cl CHSW/BR CH4 ..... 37 G6
Signal Ct CHNE CH2 .... 3 K2
Silverbirch Cft CHSW/BR CH4 47 F1
Silver Birch Wy CHSW/BR CH4 47 F1
Silverdale Av MOLD/BUCK CH7 35 H4
Silverstone Dr
   MOLD/BUCK CH7 .... 34 B6
Simonstone Rd CHSW/BR CH4 37 H5
Simpson Cl CHNE CH2 .... 19 J5
Simpson Rd CHNE CH2 .... 19 J5
Simpsons Wy CHSW/BR CH4 . 47 F1
Sixth Av CQ CH5 .... 16 C5
   CQ CH5 .... 13 C4
Skip's La CHSE CH3 .... 41 G3
Slack La CQ CH5 .... 35 J5
Smithy Cl CH/BCN CH1 .... 18 A5
Smithy La CQ CH5 .... 34 E1
   CQ CH5 .... 24 B3
Smity Pathway
   CHSW/BR CH4 .... 39 F6
Snowdon Av CHNE CH2 .... 34 A4
Snowdon Cres CHSW/BR CH4 14 E5
Somerford Rd CHSW/BR CH4 . 37 G6
Somerset Av CHNE CH2 .... 28 E1
Somerset St CHNE CH2 .... 2 E1
Sorrel Cl CHSE CH3 .... 40 C4
Souter's La CH/BCN CH1 .... 3 G1
South Av CHNE CH2 .... 30 C6
South Bank CQ CH5 .... 29 J4
   CQ CH5 .... 25 K4
South Crescent Rd
   CHSW/BR CH4 .... 3 C6
South Fields Cl
   MOLD/BUCK CH7 .... 34 C5
South Gn CQ CH5 .... 26 E2
South La MOLD/BUCK CH7 .... 34 C5
South Vw CHNE CH2 .... 30 A1
South Vw CHSW/BR CH4 ...... 39 K3
   CQ CH5 .... 44 E1
South View Rd CH/BCN CH1 ... 2 B3
Sovereign Wy CH/BCN CH1 ... 28 E6
Sparks Cl CHSE CH3 .... 40 D5
Speedwell Cl CHSE CH3 .... 40 C4
Spenser Cl CQ CH5 .... 35 H3
Spital Wk CHNE CH2 .... 3 J3
Spon Gn MOLD/BUCK CH7 ... 45 F1
Spring Dl CQ CH5 .... 35 J1
Springfield CQ CH5 .... 36 A2
Springfield Cl CHSW/BR CH4 . 46 D4
   CQ CH5 .... 24 E2
Springfield Ct CHNE CH2 ...... 30 A4
   MOLD/BUCK CH7 .... 2 B3
Springfields CHNE CH2 .... 21 G6
   HLYW CH8 .... 7 J1
Spring St CQ CH5 .... 25 K2
Springwood Cl CH/BCN CH1 .. 28 C4
The Square MOLD/BUCK CH7 45 F1
   CHSE CH3 .... 41 G2
   MOLD/BUCK CH7 * 48 A5
Stafford Rd CHNE CH2 .... 26 D1
Stainton Gv CQ CH5 .... 14 E6
Stamford La CHNE CH2 .... 21 H6
Stamford St CH/BCN CH1 ...... 28 E2
Stamford Wy CHNE CH2 .... 21 H6
   HLYW CH8 .... 8 B5
Standard Rd MOLD/BUCK CH7 35 F3
Stanley Rd MOLD/BUCK CH7 . 34 D4
Stanley Park Cl CHSW/BR CH4 38 E4
Stanley Park Dr CHSW/BR CH4 38 E5
   CQ CH5 .... 24 C4
Stanley Place CH/BCN CH1 .... 2 C4
Stanley Place Ms CH/BCN CH1 * 2 C5
Stanley Rd CH/BCN CH1 .... 29 F5
Stanley St CH/BCN CH1 .... 29 F5
   MOLD/BUCK CH7 .... 43 F3
Stanton Dr CHNE CH2 .... 30 A5
Stanton Rd CHSW/BR CH4 .... 39 K4
Stapleton Av CHSW/BR CH4 .. 48 A6
Station Ap MOLD/BUCK CH7 .. 23 H3
Station La CHNE CH2 .... 31 H2

   CO CH5 .... 36 A2
Station Rd CH/BCN CH1 .... 3 G1
   CHNE CH2 .... 19 H3
   CQ CH5 .... 36 A2
   FLINT CH6 .... 9 H4
   HLYW CH8 .... 8 A3
Station Vw CHNE CH2 .... 3 J3
Station Wy CHSW/BR CH4 ..... 45 J4
Steam Mill St CH/BCN CH1 ..... 3 G1
Stearns Cl CH/BCN CH1 .... 29 G3
Steele St CH/BCN CH1 .... 2 E5
Stendall Rd CH/BCN CH1 ...... 29 G5
Stephen Gray Rd
   MOLD/BUCK CH7 .... 43 H4
Steven Ct CHSE CH3 .... 3 H3
Stile End CHNE CH2 .... 21 H6
Stirling Ct CHSE CH3 .... 30 C6
Stocks Av CHSE CH3 .... 30 D5
Stocks La CHSE CH3 .... 40 C1
Stone Cft CHSE CH3 .... 40 D2
Stone Pl CHNE CH2 .... 40 D2
Stoneleigh Cl CQ CH5 .... 26 D2
Stone Pl CHNE CH2 .... 30 B5
Strand Cl HLYW CH8 .... 8 A2
Strand Crs HLYW CH8 .... 8 A2
Strand La HLYW CH8 .... 8 A2
Strand Rd CHSW/BR CH4 .... 8 A3
Strand Wk HLYW CH8 .... 8 A3
Stratford Rd CHNE CH2 .... 28 E4
Strawberry Flds CHSE CH3 .... 40 D5
Strawberry La CH/BCN CH1 ... 28 E1
The Street CHNE CH2 .... 30 E1
Strickland St CQ CH5 .... 25 K3
Stroyd Henardd
   MOLD/BUCK CH7 .... 43 F3
Stryd Teheingl FLINT CH6 .... 9 J5
Stryd-y-Capel (Chapel St)
   MOLD/BUCK CH7 .... 43 F3
Stryt Isa WRX/GR/LL LL12 ..... 51 J4
Stryt Isaf CHSW/BR CH4 .... 51 G1
Stuart Cl CHSE CH3 .... 30 E5
Stuart Pl CH/BCN CH1 .... 3 F2
Stubbs Pl CH/BCN CH1 .... 29 G5
Summerdale Rd CQ CH5 .... 35 J4
Summerfield Cl CHSE CH3 .... 40 E1
Summerhill Cl CHSE CH3 ...... 31 H5
Summerville Cl CQ CH5 .... 25 F1
Summer Rd CH/BCN CH1 ...... 28 E4
Sumpter Pathway CHNE CH2 . 30 B5
Sunbury Crs CHSW/BR CH4 ... 39 F4
Sundawn Av HLYW CH8 .... 8 B5
Sunningdale MOLD/BUCK CH7 34 C4
Sunnside Cl FLINT CH6 .... 8 D2
Sunny Rdg MOLD/BUCK CH7 . 42 E1
Sunnyside CQ CH5 .... 26 B6
Surrey Rd CHNE CH2 .... 28 E1
Suspension Br CH/BCN CH1 .... 3 G5
Swinchiard La FLINT CH6 ...... 13 C3
Swinchiard Wk FLINT CH6 ..... 13 C3
Swinleys Hey CHSE CH3 .... 40 C3
Swn-y-Gwynt FLINT CH6 .... 13 H5
Swn-y-Nant MOLD/BUCK CH7 43 F4
Swn y Nant MOLD/BUCK CH7 * 43 F4
Sycamore Av CQ CH5 .... 35 H3
Sycamore Cl CQ CH5 .... 35 H3
   MOLD/BUCK CH7 .... 50 A1
Sycamore Gv CHSW/BR CH4 . 47 F1
Sydney Rd CH/BCN CH1 .... 3 G1
Sydney St FLINT CH6 .... 13 G2
Sydney Wk FLINT CH6 .... 13 G3

T

Tabernacle St MOLD/BUCK CH7 34 D6
Talbot St CH/BCN CH1 .... 3 F1
Talfryn Cl CQ CH5 .... 15 F5
Talgarreg Dr CQ CH5 .... 24 E2
Taliesin Av CQ CH5 .... 25 J2
Tan-y-Bryn HLYW CH8 .... 5 G5
   MOLD/BUCK CH7 .... 33 G4
Tan-y-Boed HLYW CH8 .... 7 G1
Tan-y-Coed MOLD/BUCK CH7 42 E3
Tan-y-Felin HLYW CH8 .... 5 G2
Tan-y-Graig MOLD/BUCK CH7 42 D3
Tan y Lloc La HLYW CH8 .... 6 B1
Tan-yr-Ysgol MOLD/BUCK CH7 33 G4
Tarrant Ct CH/BCN CH1 .... 30 E5
Tarvin Rd CHSE CH3 .... 40 E5
Tatton Cl CHSW/BR CH4 .... 38 E5
Taylors Vw CQ CH5 .... 25 J4
Taynton Cl CQ CH5 .... 24 E6
Tecwyn Dr CQ CH5 .... 14 E6
Tegid Wy CHSW/BR CH4 .... 38 D5
Telford Wy CHSW/BR CH4 ..... 39 F4
Tennyson Wk CHNE CH2 .... 29 G3
Tenth Av CQ CH5 .... 16 B5
Terrace La CHSW/BR CH4 ..... 46 E6
Terrig Crs MOLD/BUCK CH7 .. 34 D6
Terrig St CQ CH5 .... 25 K4
Tewksbury Cl CHNE CH2 .... 30 B1
Thackeray Dr CHNE CH2 .... 29 G3
Third Av CQ CH5 .... 16 D5
   FLINT CH6 .... 13 G4
Thirlmere Rd CHNE CH2 .... 30 C3
Thomas Av CQ CH5 .... 35 G2
Thomas Brassey Cl CHNE CH2 29 F2
Thomas Cl CH/BCN CH1 .... 28 E2
   FLINT CH6 .... 21 H6
Thomas St FLINT CH6 .... 13 G2
Thornberry Cl CH/BCN CH1 ... 28 E5
Thornfield Av CQ CH5 .... 35 H2
Thornfields CQ CH5 .... 25 J4
Thornhill Cl CHSW/BR CH4 ... 46 D1
Thornton Dr CHNE CH2 .... 29 K3
Threos Cl CQ CH5 .... 35 J4
Thurston Rd CHNE CH2 .... 34 E5
Tilers Cl MOLD/BUCK CH7 .... 34 C5
Timberfields Rd CH/BCN CH1 18 A6

Tintern Av CHNE CH2 ...... 30 B2
Tir Wat MOLD/BUCK CH7 ...... 34 A6
Titian Cl CQ CH5 ...... 14 E6
Tivaton Cl CQ CH5 ...... 35 F2
Tiverton Cl CHNE CH2 ...... 30 A3
Toft Cl CHSW/BR CH4 ...... 38 E5
Toll Bar Rd CHSE CH3 ...... 40 E1
Tollemache Ter CHNE CH2 ...... 3 K5
Tomkinson St CHNE CH2 ...... 3 H1
Toogood Cl CHNE CH2 ...... 21 H6
Totland Gv CHNE CH2 ...... 30 A4
Tower Cots MOLD/BUCK CH7 * 43 G6
Towergate CH/BCN CH1 ...... 2 B5
Tower Rd CH/BCN CH1 ...... 2 B5
Towers Wy CHSW/BR CH4 ...... 45 J4
Townfield La CH/BCN CH1 ...... 18 D2
Trafford St CH/BCN CH1 ...... 2 E1
Tram La MOLD/BUCK CH7 ...... 34 E5
Tram Rd MOLD/BUCK CH7 ...... 34 E4
Trebor Av FLINT CH6 ...... 9 H6
Treborth Rd CH/BCN CH1 ...... 28 D5
Trefoil Cl CHSE CH3 ...... 40 D4
Tregele Cl CH/BCN CH1 ...... 28 D5
Trelawny Av FLINT CH6 ...... 13 H3
Trelech CQ CH5 ...... 24 E4
Trem Afon MOLD/BUCK CH7 ...... 43 G5
Trem-y-Foel MOLD/BUCK CH7 * 35 C5
Trinity Rd HLYW CH8 ...... 5 C6
Trinity St CH/BCN CH1 ...... 2 D4
Tros-yr-Aber HLYW CH8 ...... 5 F6
Trueman's Ct CQ CH5 ...... 36 A2
Trueman's Wy CQ CH5 ...... 36 A1
Trum-yr-Hydref
  MOLD/BUCK CH7 ...... 24 C4
Tudor Av FLINT CH6 ...... 13 G5
Tudor Cl CQ CH5 ...... 25 K3
  HLYW CH8 ...... 7 K3
  MOLD/BUCK CH7 ...... 24 B4
Tudor Ct WRX/GR/LL LL12 ...... 51 H4
Tudor Wy CHSE CH3 ...... 40 C3
Tuscan Wy CQ CH5 ...... 15 G6
Tushingham Cl CHSE CH3 ...... 40 D5
Twain Cl CQ CH5 ...... 35 G2
Tyddyn Mesham FLINT CH6 ...... 9 J6
Tyddyn St MOLD/BUCK CH7 ...... 43 F3
Tyn Twll La FLINT CH6 ...... 8 E3

U

Ullswater Crs CHNE CH2 ...... 30 C2
Ullswater Rd MOLD/BUCK CH7 ...... 34 E4
Union St CH/BCN CH1 ...... 3 G4
Union Ter CH/BCN CH1 ...... 3 F5
Uplands Av CQ CH5 ...... 25 F3
Upper Aston Hall La CQ CH5 ...... 35 K1
Upper Bryn Coch (Bryn Coch
  Uchaf) MOLD/BUCK CH7 ...... 42 D4
Upper Bryn Rd CQ CH5 ...... 15 F6
Upper Cambrian Rd
  CH/BCN CH1 ...... 2 B2
Upper Northgate St
  CH/BCN CH1 ...... 2 D1
Upper River Bank FLINT CH6 ...... 8 D1
Upton Cl CHNE CH2 ...... 29 J2
Upton La CHNE CH2 ...... 29 J1
Upton Pk CHNE CH2 ...... 29 K2
Uwch-y-Dre MOLD/BUCK CH7 ...... 42 B5
Uwch-y-Mor HLYW CH8 ...... 11 H4
Uwch-y-Nant MOLD/BUCK CH7 ...... 43 K2

V

Vale Av CQ CH5 ...... 35 G3

Vale Cl CHSW/BR CH4 ...... 47 G1
Vale Dr MOLD/BUCK CH7 ...... 43 K5
Valley Dr CHNE CH2 ...... 29 H3
Vaughans La CHSE CH3 ...... 40 C2
Vaughan Wy CQ CH5 ...... 25 F4
Venable's Rd CH/BCN CH1 ...... 29 F4
Vermeer Cl CQ CH5 ...... 14 E6
Vernon Rd CH/BCN CH1 ...... 2 B3
The Vetches CHSE CH3 ...... 31 H3
Vicarage Cl CHSE CH3 ...... 31 H3
Vicarage Dr FLINT CH6 ...... 9 H6
Vicarage Rd CHNE CH2 ...... 30 B5
  ...... 9 H5
Vicars Cross Rd CHSE CH3 ...... 30 D6
Vicar's La CH/BCN CH1 ...... 3 F5
Vickers Cl CQ CH5 ...... 26 A5
Victoria Av MOLD/BUCK CH7 ...... 34 E5
Victoria Ct CHNE CH2 ...... 29 J5
Victoria Crs CHSW/BR CH4 ...... 3 G6
  CQ CH5 ...... 25 J2
  MOLD/BUCK CH7 ...... 50 B5
Victoria Pk FLINT CH6 * 8 D2
Victoria Pathway
  CHSW/BR CH4 ...... 3 G7
Victoria Pl CH/BCN CH1 ...... 2 E5
  CHNE CH2 ...... 18 A3
Victoria Rd CH/BCN CH1 ...... 2 E2
  CHNE CH2 ...... 29 J5
  CHSW/BR CH4 ...... 38 D4
  CQ CH5 ...... 25 J2
  FLINT CH6 ...... 8 E2
  MOLD/BUCK CH7 ...... 34 E5
  MOLD/BUCK CH7 ...... 43 F3
Victoria Ter MOLD/BUCK CH7 ...... 48 G2
Victory Ct MOLD/BUCK CH7 ...... 43 G4
Viking Wy CQ CH5 ...... 14 E6
Village Rd CHSE CH3 ...... 41 G2
Villa Rd CQ CH5 ...... 27 F2
Vincent Dr CHSW/BR CH4 ...... 39 H4
Virginia Dr CH/BCN CH1 ...... 28 C5
Volunteer St CH/BCN CH1 ...... 2 E4
Vounog Hl CHSW/BR CH4 ...... 45 J5
Vownog MOLD/BUCK CH7 ...... 33 G3
Vownog Newydd
  MOLD/BUCK CH7 ...... 33 H3
Vyrnwy Rd CHSW/BR CH4 ...... 38 D4

W

Walker St CHNE CH2 ...... 3 H1
Walls Av CH/BCN CH1 ...... 2 B4
Walnut Cl CHNE CH2 ...... 29 K1
  CHSW/BR CH4 ...... 45 J4
Walpole Av CQ CH5 ...... 35 J2
Walpole St CH/BCN CH1 ...... 2 C1
Walter St CH/BCN CH1 ...... 3 F1
Waltham Pl CHSW/BR CH4 * 39 G4
Walton Pl CH/BCN CH1 ...... 28 E4
The Waltons CHSW/BR CH4 ...... 40 A4
Wards Ter CHNE CH2 ...... 3 J1
Wared Dr MOLD/BUCK CH7 ...... 24 B4
Warkick Rd CH/BCN CH1 ...... 29 F3
Warren Crs MOLD/BUCK CH7 ...... 35 H6
Warren Dr CHSW/BR CH4 ...... 46 E1
Warrington Rd CHNE CH2 ...... 30 D3
Washington Dr CQ CH5 ...... 35 J1
Watergate Rw North
  CH/BCN CH1 ...... 2 D4
Watergate Rw South
  CH/BCN CH1 ...... 2 D5
Watergate Sq CH/BCN CH1 ...... 2 B5
Watergate St CH/BCN CH1 ...... 2 D5
Waterloo Rd CHNE CH2 ...... 29 J4
Waters Edge CH/BCN CH1 ...... 2 B5
Waterside CH/BCN CH1 ...... 2 E5
Waters Reams CHSE CH3 ...... 40 D2

Water St MOLD/BUCK CH7 ...... 43 F3
Water Tower St CH/BCN CH1 ...... 2 D3
Watertower Vw CHNE CH2 ...... 3 K5
Waterway CHSE CH3 ...... 41 K5
Watkin St CQ CH5 ...... 26 E5
Watling Crs CHSW/BR CH4 ...... 40 A3
Wat's Dyke Av HLYW CH8 ...... 8 A2
Wats Dyke Av MOLD/BUCK CH7 ...... 34 A5
Wat's Dyke Wy
  MOLD/BUCK CH7 ...... 33 H3
Watson's Cl CHSW/BR CH4 ...... 47 G1
Watt's Rd CHSE CH3 ...... 45 J5
Watts Ct MOLD/BUCK CH7 ...... 34 B6
Wavells Wy CHSE CH3 ...... 40 D5
Waverley Ter CHNE CH2 ...... 30 A5
Wavertree Mill Quays CHSE CH3 41 K5
Wavertree Rd CHSE CH3 ...... 28 C3
Wayside Ct CHNE CH2 ...... 21 H6
Wealstone Ct CHNE CH2 ...... 30 A3
Weal Stone La CHNE CH2 ...... 30 A2
Weaver Gv CHNE CH2 ...... 21 H5
Weaver St CH/BCN CH1 ...... 2 D5
Webster Cl CHNE CH2 ...... 47 G1
Wedgewood Hts HLYW CH8 ...... 7 J2
Wedgwood Rd CQ CH5 * 25 F5
Weighbridge Rd CQ CH5 ...... 15 H2
Welland Dr CQ CH5 ...... 25 F1
Well House Dr CHSW/BR CH4 ...... 45 K3
Wellington Cl CH/BCN CH1 ...... 2 E2
Wellington Rd CHSW/BR CH4 ...... 47 F1
Wellington St CQ CH5 ...... 25 K2
Well La CH/BCN CH1 ...... 19 F5
  CHSE CH3 ...... 30 A4
Wells Cl CHNE CH2 ...... 21 H6
Well St HLYW CH8 ...... 8 A2
  MOLD/BUCK CH7 ...... 44 B1
Welsh Rd CHSW/BR CH4 * 47 K3
  CQ CH5 ...... 26 C2
Wemyss Rd CH/BCN CH1 ...... 28 D4
Wenlock Crs CQ CH5 ...... 26 C5
Wenlock Wy CHSW/BR CH4 ...... 39 H4
Wentworth Cl MOLD/BUCK CH7 34 C4
Wepre Ct CQ CH5 ...... 25 F3
Wepre Dr CQ CH5 ...... 25 J1
Wepre Hall Crs CQ CH5 ...... 25 G2
Wepre La CQ CH5 ...... 24 D4
Wepre Pk CQ CH5 ...... 25 H3
Wern Av FLINT CH6 ...... 9 H5
Wern Ucha FLINT CH6 ...... 9 G5
Wervin Rd CHNE CH2 ...... 20 B5
Wesley St CQ CH5 ...... 15 H6
West Bank CH/BCN CH1 ...... 29 J4
Westbourne Crs
  MOLD/BUCK CH7 ...... 34 C6
Westbourne Rd CH/BCN CH1 ...... 29 J4
Westbrook Dr
  CH/BCN CH1 ...... 44 E1
Westbury Dr MOLD/BUCK CH7 ...... 35 G6
Westbury Wy MOLD/BUCK CH7 ...... 39 H4
West Dr HLYW CH8 ...... 7 K3
Western Ap CHNE CH2 ...... 30 A4
Western Av CH/BCN CH1 ...... 28 D5
Western Ct CHNE CH2 ...... 30 A4
Westfield Cl CHSW/BR CH4 ...... 39 J4
Westfield Dr CHSW/BR CH4 ...... 45 H5
West Lorne St CH/BCN CH1 ...... 2 C2
Westminster Av CHSW/BR CH4 ...... 39 H4
Westminster Cl CHNE CH2 ...... 3 J2
Westminster Crs CQ CH5 ...... 25 K3
Westminster Rd CHNE CH2 ...... 3 J1
  CHSW/BR CH4 ...... 38 D5
Westminster Ter CHSW/BR CH4 ...... 39 J3
Weston Cl CQ CH5 ...... 26 D2
Weston Gv CHNE CH2 ...... 30 A2
West St CHNE CH2 ...... 30 A5
West Vw CHSW/BR CH4 ...... 45 J6
  MOLD/BUCK CH7 ...... 45 J5
  MOLD/BUCK CH7 ...... 44 E1

West View Dr MOLD/BUCK CH7 .. 43 J3
Westward Rd CHSE CH3 ...... 40 C2
Westway CQ CH5 ...... 26 C6
Wetherby Cl CH/BCN CH1 ...... 2 A2
Weybourne Cl CHSW/BR CH4 * .. 38 E5
Whaddon Dr CHSW/BR CH4 ...... 39 F6
Wharfdale Av CQ CH5 ...... 25 F2
Wharton St CHNE CH2 ...... 3 J3
Wheldon Cl CHNE CH2 ...... 20 A6
Whipcord La CH/BCN CH1 ...... 2 A2
Whitby Av CHNE CH2 ...... 29 K3
Whitchurch Rd CHSE CH3 ...... 40 D1
Whitecroft Cl CQ CH5 ...... 24 B1
White Farm Rd
  MOLD/BUCK CH7 ...... 34 C3
White Friars CH/BCN CH1 ...... 2 D5
White La CHSE CH3 ...... 41 F2
White Oaks Dr
  CHSW/BR CH4 ...... 24 C4
Whites Meadow CHSE CH3 ...... 40 C5
White Way Cv CQ CH5 ...... 26 D2
Whitford St HLYW CH8 ...... 7 K2
Whitrock Rd CHSW/BR CH4 ...... 45 K3
Whittle Cl CQ CH5 ...... 26 E5
Whitton Dr CHNE CH2 ...... 30 A3
Wicker La CHSE CH3 ...... 31 J4
The Wiend CHNE CH2 ...... 29 K4
The Wigdale CQ CH5 ...... 36 A2
Wilbraham Ct CHNE CH2 ...... 21 H6
Willam Rd CH/BCN CH1 ...... 28 D4
Williams Cl CHNE CH2 ...... 29 J4
  CHSW/BR CH4 ...... 45 K3
William St CH/BCN CH1 ...... 2 E2
  CHSE CH3 ...... 3 J1
Willoway Rd CHSE CH3 ...... 30 D6
Willow Cl CQ CH5 ...... 26 C4
Willow Cl (Llys Helyg)
  MOLD/BUCK CH7 ...... 35 G6
Willow Crs CHNE CH2 ...... 30 C4
  CQ CH5 ...... 35 H2
Willow Dr CHNE CH2 ...... 28 D5
  FLINT CH6 ...... 12 E4
Willow Gv CHNE CH2 ...... 30 D4
Willow Gv (Llwyn Helig)
  MOLD/BUCK CH7 ...... 34 C3
Willowherb Cl CHSE CH3 ...... 40 C4
Willow La CQ CH5 ...... 26 C4
Willow Lea CH/BCN CH1 ...... 19 K6
Willow Rd CHSW/BR CH4 ...... 39 F4
The Willow MOLD/BUCK CH7 ...... 34 D3
Willow Wk MOLD/BUCK CH7 ...... 50 A1
Willow Wy CHSW/BR CH4 ...... 47 F1
Wilton Rd CQ CH5 ...... 26 B6
Winchester Sq CHSW/BR CH4 ...... 39 F6
Windermere Av CHNE CH2 ...... 30 C2
  CQ CH5 ...... 25 H1
Windmill Cl HLYW CH8 ...... 8 B3
  MOLD/BUCK CH7 ...... 34 D5
Windmill La CHNE CH2 ...... 41 F2
Windmill Ri CHNE CH2 ...... 29 K1
Windmill Rd MOLD/BUCK CH7 ...... 34 D5
Windsor Av CQ CH5 ...... 25 H2
  WRX/GR/LL LL12 ...... 51 H6
Windsor Cl CHNE CH2 ...... 48 E1
  FLINT CH6 ...... 12 E5
Windsor Pk HLYW CH8 ...... 7 K3
Windsor Rd CHSW/BR CH4 ...... 39 F4
Winkwell Dr CHSW/BR CH4 ...... 39 G5
Winscombe Dr CHSE CH3 ...... 30 E6
Winsford Wy CH/BCN CH1 ...... 29 F6
Wirral Vw CQ CH5 ...... 25 K3
Withy Cft CHSE CH3 ...... 40 D3
Woburn Dr CHNE CH2 ...... 30 B1
Wold Ct CQ CH5 ...... 36 A2
Woodbank La CH/BCN CH1 ...... 17 H1
Woodbank Rd CQ CH5 ...... 25 G2
Wood Cft CHSE CH3 ...... 31 H4
Woodcroft Rd

  MOLD/BUCK CH7 35
Woodfield Av FLINT CH6 13
Woodfield Cl CHSW/BR CH4 46
  CQ CH5 25
Woodfield Gv CHNE CH2 30
Wood Gn MOLD/BUCK CH7 45
Woodgrove MOLD/BUCK CH7 50
Woodland Bank CHNE CH2 21
Woodland Ct FLINT CH6 13
Woodland Crs CQ CH5 * 25
Woodland Dr FLINT CH6 13
  HLYW CH8 5
Woodlands Cl MOLD/BUCK CH7 .. 43
  CQ CH5 36
Woodlands Dr CHNE CH2 30
  CQ CH5 35
Woodlands La CHSE CH3 30
Woodlands Rd CHSE CH3 40
  CHSW/BR CH4 38
The Woodlands CQ CH5 35
Woodland St CQ CH5 25
Wood La CHSW/BR CH4 37
  CQ CH5 35
  CQ CH5 35
  8
Woodlea Av CHNE CH2 30
Woodside Cl CQ CH5 35
Woodside Rd CH/BCN CH1 28
Wood St CQ CH5 26
Wood Ville CQ CH5 25
Worcester Pl CH/BCN CH1 35
Wordsworth Cl CQ CH5 35
Wordsworth Crs CH/BCN CH1 29
Wordsworth Ms CH/BCN CH1 29
Wordsworth Sq CH/BCN CH1 29
Worsley Av CH/BCN CH1 18
Wrekin Wy CHSW/BR CH4 39
Wrexham Rd CHSW/BR CH4 39
  CHSW/BR CH4 45
  CHSW/BR CH4 49
  MOLD/BUCK CH7 43
Wrexham St MOLD/BUCK CH7 .. 43
Wroxham Cl CHNE CH2 2
Wycliffe Ct CHNE CH2 30
Wylfa Av MOLD/BUCK CH7 43
Wyndham Rd CH/BCN CH1 28
Wynnstay Rd CHSW/BR CH4 37

Y

Yarrow Cl CHSW/BR CH4 47
Y Cedrwydd (The Cedars)
  MOLD/BUCK CH7 34
Y Dolydd MOLD/BUCK CH7 42
Y Dreflan HLYW CH8 7
Yerburgh St CHNE CH2 29
Yew Tree Av CH/BCN CH1 27
Yew Tree Cl CHSW/BR CH4 47
Ygerddi HLYW CH8 4
Y Glrfach MOLD/BUCK CH7 43
The Yonne CH/BCN CH1 2
York Av CQ CH5 25
York Dr CHNE CH2 21
York Rd CQ CH5 14
York St CH/BCN CH1 3
Yowley Rd CQ CH5 35
Yr Aber HLYW CH8 5
Yr Ydlan MOLD/BUCK CH7 43
Y Waen FLINT CH6 23

Index - featured places

Abbey Gate School
  CHNE CH2 ...... 2 D1
Abbots Lane Primary School
  CHSW/BR CH4 ...... 45 J5
Acorn Business Park
  FLINT CH6 ...... 13 F2
Acresfield Primary School
  CHNE CH2 ...... 20 B6
Alun School
  MOLD/BUCK CH7 ...... 43 F4
Arches Community
  Primary School
  CH/BCN CH1 ...... 28 E3
Argoed High School
  MOLD/BUCK CH7 ...... 34 A4
Ashmount Industrial Centre
  FLINT CH6 ...... 13 G2
Basingwerk Abbey (ruins)
  HLYW CH8 ...... 5 G6
Beaufort Park Hotel
  MOLD/BUCK CH7 ...... 33 J5
Belgrave Infant School
  CHSW/BR CH4 ...... 39 H5
Belmont Infant School
  MOLD/BUCK CH7 ...... 34 C6
Best Western
  The Queen Hotel
  CH/BCN CH1 ...... 3 H2
Best Western
  Westminster Hotel
  CH/BCN CH1 ...... 3 G2
Bishop (Bluecoat) CE
  High School
  CHSE CH3 ...... 40 C2
Blacon Clinic
  CH/BCN CH1 ...... 28 E3
Blacon County High School
  CH/BCN CH1 ...... 28 D4
The Borders Industrial Park
  CHSW/BR CH4 ...... 38 C3

Boughton Health Centre
  CHNE CH2 ...... 3 J3
Boughton Heath
  Primary School
  CHSE CH3 ...... 40 D2
Boughton St Pauls
  Infants School
  CHSE CH3 ...... 3 H3
The Bridgegate
  CH/BCN CH1 ...... 2 E6
British Aerospace
  Aircraft Factory
  CHSW/BR CH4 ...... 37 H4
Bromfield Industrial Estate
  MOLD/BUCK CH7 ...... 43 G4
Broncoed Business Park
  MOLD/BUCK CH7 ...... 43 G5
Brookside Hotel
  CHNE CH2 ...... 29 K4
Broughton Industrial Estate
  CHSW/BR CH4 ...... 37 K4
Broughton J & I School
  CHSW/BR CH4 ...... 37 G6
Broughton Shopping Park
  CHSW/BR CH4 ...... 37 J6
Brymau Four Trading Estate
  CHSW/BR CH4 ...... 38 D3
Brymau One Trading Estate
  CHSW/BR CH4 ...... 38 E3
Brymau Three
  Trading Estate
  CHSW/BR CH4 ...... 38 E3
Brymau Two Trading Estate
  CHSW/BR CH4 ...... 38 E3
Bryn Coch Primary School
  MOLD/BUCK CH7 ...... 43 F3
Bryn Deva Primary School
  CQ CH5 ...... 15 F6
Brynford Primary School
  HLYW CH8 ...... 7 J6

Bryn Pennant Primary School
  HLYW CH8 ...... 4 A1
Buckley CC
  MOLD/BUCK CH7 ...... 35 F6
Buckley Cemetery
  MOLD/BUCK CH7 ...... 34 D5
Buckley Health Centre
  MOLD/BUCK CH7 ...... 34 D6
Cambrian Business Park
  MOLD/BUCK CH7 ...... 43 H5
Carmel Primary School
  HLYW CH8 ...... 7 F1
Castell Alun High School
  WRX/GR/LL LL12 ...... 51 J4
Castle Park Industrial Estate
  FLINT CH6 ...... 13 G1
Catharalls Industrial Estate
  MOLD/BUCK CH7 ...... 34 D3
The Catholic High
  School Chester
  CHSW/BR CH4 ...... 39 J4
Cherry Grove Primary School
  CHSE CH3 ...... 40 C1
Cheshire County Officers
  Sports Club
  CHNE CH2 ...... 30 C2
The Cheshire Military Museum
  CH/BCN CH1 ...... 2 D6
Chester Amphitheatre
  CH/BCN CH1 ...... 3 F5
Chesterbank Business Park
  CHSW/BR CH4 ...... 38 D3
Chester Boughton Hall CC
  CHSE CH3 ...... 40 D1
Chester Business Centre
  CH/BCN CH1 ...... 3 F4
Chester Business Park
  CHSW/BR CH4 ...... 49 J1
Chester Castle
  CH/BCN CH1 ...... 2 D7

Chester Cathedral
  CH/BCN CH1 ...... 2 E3
Chester City FC (Deva Stadium)
  CH/BCN CH1 ...... 38 E1
Chester College of Law
  CHSE CH3 ...... 41 F2
Chester Crematorium
  CH/BCN CH1 ...... 29 G4
Chester Figure Clinic
  CH/BCN CH1 ...... 2 E5
Chester General Cemetery
  CHSW/BR CH4 ...... 39 J3
Chester Golf Club
  CHSW/BR CH4 ...... 2 A6
The Chester Grosvenor Hotel
  CH/BCN CH1 ...... 2 E4
Chester History
  & Heritage Centre
  CH/BCN CH1 ...... 2 E5
Chester Racecourse
  CH/BCN CH1 ...... 2 B6
Chester Retail Park
  CH/BCN CH1 ...... 29 G6
Chester Rugby Union FC
  CHSE CH3 ...... 31 F6
Chester Southerly
  Touring Park
  CHSW/BR CH4 ...... 48 C3
Chester Toy Museum
  CH/BCN CH1 ...... 2 E5
Chester West
  Employment Park
  CH/BCN CH1 ...... 28 E6
Chester Zoo
  CHNE CH2 ...... 20 A5
Christleton County
  High School
  CHSE CH3 ...... 41 G3
Christleton Primary School
  CHSE CH3 ...... 41 F2

Christleton Sports Centre
  CHSE CH3 41
Christleton Sports Club
  CHSE CH3 41
City Walls Medical Centre
  CH/BCN CH1 2
Connah's Quay Cemetery
  CQ CH5 15
Connah's Quay High School
  CQ CH5 14
Connah's Quay Sports Centre
  CQ CH5 14
Cornist Park CP School
  FLINT CH6 12
Countess of Chester
  Hospital
  CHNE CH2 29
Crowne Plaza Hotel
  CH/BCN CH1 3
The Curzon Hotel
  CH/BCN CH1 3
Custom House Lane
  Primary School
  CQ CH5 15
Dee Bank Industrial Estate
  CQ CH5 15
Dee Banks Special School
  CHSE CH3 30
Dee Point CP School
  CH/BCN CH1 28
Dee Road Infant School
  CQ CH5 25
Deeside College
  FLINT CH6 16
  MOLD/BUCK CH7 43
Deeside College Corus
  Learning Centre
  CQ CH5 15
Deeside Community Hospital
  CQ CH5 25

-eside Industrial Estate
  CO CH5 ...... 16 E5
-eside Stadium
  CO CH5 ...... 14 E5
-yn & Deeside
  Business Centre
  CO CH5 ...... 35 G1
-e Hotel
  CHNE CH2 ...... 30 B4
-wen Foundation
  Primary School
  CHSW/BR CH4 ...... 46 E4
-a Business Park
  CO CH5 ...... 16 E6
-a Industrial Estate
  CO CH5 ...... 26 D4
-Vere St David's Park Hotel
  CH 35 H1
-a Roman Experience
  CH/BCN CH1 ...... 2 D5
-shill Hospital
  CO CH5 ...... 45 H1
-lleston CE Primary School
  CHSW/BR CH4 ...... 48 A5
-in Park Special School
  CHNE CH2 ...... 29 K2
-ry Industrial Estate
  CO CH5 ...... 35 G4
-ry Primary School
  MOLD/BUCK CH7 ...... 35 H5
-nkirk Trading Estate
  CH/BCN CH1 ...... 18 D1
-leston CE Primary School
  CHSW/BR CH4 ...... 49 K2
-d High School
  MOLD/BUCK CH7 ...... 34 D5
-s Medical Centre
  CO CH5 ...... 30 A5
-oe Castle
  ...... 25 F5
-oe Green Primary School
  CHNE CH2 ...... 35 G1
-essway Business Park
  CO CH5 ...... 26 C3
-Firs School
  CHNE CH2 ...... 30 A3
-t Castle
  FLINT CH6 ...... 13 H2
-t Child Health Clinic
  FLINT CH6 ...... 13 H3
-t Community Hospital
  FLINT CH6 ...... 13 F3
-t FC
  FLINT CH6 ...... 13 G5
-t Golf Club
  FLINT CH6 ...... 12 D4
-t High School
  FLINT CH6 ...... 13 G5
-t Leisure Centre
  FLINT CH6 ...... 13 G2
-t Mountain
  Primary School
  FLINT CH6 ...... 23 G2
-tshire Retail Park
  FLINT CH6 ...... 13 F2
-Forum Shopping Centre
  CH/BCN CH1 ...... 2 D4
-den City Industrial Estate
  CO CH5 ...... 16 D6
-den Lane Medical Centre
  CH/BCN CH1 ...... 2 C2
-Gateway To Wales Hotel
  CO CH5 ...... 26 D1
-t Aber Primary School
  CHNE CH2 ...... 8 E2
-rafon Primary School
  MOLD/BUCK CH7 ...... 43 F4
-tyn CP School
  CO CH5 ...... 15 F6
-ater Grace School
  CHNE CH2 ...... 19 H2
-enfield Business Park 1
  HLYW CH8 ...... 5 H5
-enfield Business Park 2
  HLYW CH8 ...... 5 H5
-enfield Business Park
  HLYW CH8 ...... 8 D1
-enfield Valley Country Park
  HLYW CH8 ...... 5 G6

Greyhound Retail Park
  CH/BCN CH1 ...... 29 F5
Grosvenor Museum
  CH/BCN CH1 ...... 2 E6
Grosvenor Nuffield Hospital
  CHSW/BR CH4 ...... 39 J4
Grosvenor Shopping Centre
  CH/BCN CH1 ...... 2 E5
Guilden Sutton
  Primary School
  CHSE CH3 ...... 31 G3
Gwernymynydd
  Primary School
  MOLD/BUCK CH7 ...... 42 B5
Gwynedd Primary School
  FLINT CH6 ...... 13 G4
Hammond School
  CHNE CH2 ...... 30 E1
Handbridge Medical Centre
  CHSW/BR CH4 ...... 39 K3
Happy Feet Health Centre
  FLINT CH6 ...... 13 G2
Hawarden Airport
  ...... 37 H3
Hawarden Castle
  CO CH5 ...... 36 C3
Hawarden Golf Club
  CO CH5 ...... 35 K2
Hawarden Health Centre
  CO CH5 ...... 36 B2
Hawarden High School
  CO CH5 ...... 35 J1
Hawarden Industrial Park
  CO CH5 ...... 37 F3
Hawarden Infant School
  CO CH5 ...... 35 J1
Heath Lane Medical Centre
  CHSE CH3 ...... 40 C1
Highfield Community
  Primary School
  CHNE CH2 ...... 28 A1
Holywell Golf Club
  HLYW CH8 ...... 7 H5
Holywell High School
  HLYW CH8 ...... 8 B2
Hoole CE Primary School
  CO CH5 ...... 30 C5
Hoole Hall Hotel
  CHNE CH2 ...... 30 E3
Huntington Primary School
  CHSE CH3 ...... 40 C5
Innkeeper's Lodge
  CHNE CH2 ...... 30 E2
  ...... 41 F2
JH Godwin Primary School
  CO CH5 ...... 28 D4
John Summers High School
  CO CH5 ...... 26 A3
King Charles Tower
  CH/BCN CH1 ...... 2 E3
The Kings School
  CHSW/BR CH4 ...... 39 H6
Kus Industrial Estate
  CHNE CH2 ...... 36 E4
Lache Health Centre
  CHSW/BR CH4 ...... 39 G5
Lache Primary School
  CHSW/BR CH4 ...... 39 G5
Lakeside Business Village
  CO CH5 ...... 35 H1
Little Mountain
  Industrial Estate
  MOLD/BUCK CH7 ...... 35 G6
Lixwm Primary School
  CH/BCN CH1 ...... 2 E2
Macdonald Blossoms Hotel
  HLYW CH8 ...... 10 B6
Mancot Clinic
  CO CH5 ...... 36 B6
Manor Industrial Estate
  FLINT CH6 ...... 9 J3
Manor Lane Industrial Estate
  CO CH5 ...... 37 F4
Marches Medical Centre
  MOLD/BUCK CH7 ...... 34 D5
Megabowl
  CH/BCN CH1 ...... 29 F5

Merton House School
  CH/BCN CH1 ...... 29 J4
Mickle Trafford
  Village School
  CHNE CH2 ...... 21 G6
Mill Hotel
  CH/BCN CH1 ...... 3 G3
Mill View Primary School
  CHNE CH2 ...... 30 A2
Mold Business Park
  MOLD/BUCK CH7 ...... 43 F5
Mold CC
  MOLD/BUCK CH7 ...... 43 G2
Mold Cemetery
  MOLD/BUCK CH7 ...... 43 G3
Mold Child Health Clinic
  MOLD/BUCK CH7 ...... 43 F2
Mold Community Hospital
  MOLD/BUCK CH7 ...... 42 E2
Mold RFC
  MOLD/BUCK CH7 ...... 43 G2
Mold Sports Centre
  MOLD/BUCK CH7 ...... 43 F4
Mountain Lane
  Primary School
  MOLD/BUCK CH7 ...... 34 E5
Mountain Park Hotel
  CHNE CH2 ...... 13 F6
Mynydd Isa Junior School
  MOLD/BUCK CH7 ...... 43 K1
New Brighton Cemetery
  FLINT CH6 ...... 8 E2
The Newgate
  CH/BCN CH1 ...... 3 F5
Newton Primary School
  CHNE CH2 ...... 30 A4
Northgate Arena
  Leisure Centre
  CHNE CH2 ...... 2 D2
Northgate Medical Centre
  CH/BCN CH1 ...... 2 D2
The Northgate
  CH/BCN CH1 ...... 2 D3
Northop Golf & Country Club
  MOLD/BUCK CH7 ...... 33 H1
Northop Hall Country
  House Hotel
  MOLD/BUCK CH7 ...... 24 D5
Northop Hall Primary School
  MOLD/BUCK CH7 ...... 24 B4
Northop Road Cemetery
  FLINT CH6 ...... 13 G3
Odeon Theatre
  CH/BCN CH1 ...... 2 D3
Oldfield CP School
  CHSE CH3 ...... 30 E5
Old Padeswood Golf Club
  MOLD/BUCK CH7 ...... 44 C3
The Osteopathic
  Health Centre
  CH/BCN CH1 ...... 29 H5
Outreach Theatre
  MOLD/BUCK CH7 ...... 43 F3
Overleigh St Marys
  Primary School
  CHSW/BR CH4 ...... 39 K3
Owl Halt Industrial Estate
  CO CH5 ...... 27 F2
Padeswood & Buckley
  Golf Club
  MOLD/BUCK CH7 ...... 44 C4
Park Medical Centre
  CHNE CH2 ...... 30 B4
Parkway Business Centre
  CO CH5 ...... 16 C4
Penarlag Primary School
  CO CH5 ...... 25 J6
Pennant Park Golf Club
  ...... 4 A3
Pentre Industrial Estate
  CO CH5 ...... 26 D4
Pentrobin St John the
  Baptist VA School
  CHSW/BR CH4 ...... 45 K2
Penyffordd County
  Junior School
  CHSW/BR CH4 ...... 45 J4
Perth Y Terfyn Infant School
  HLYW CH8 ...... 8 A4

Pinfold Lane Industrial Estate
  MOLD/BUCK CH7 ...... 34 C3
Premier Inn
  CHNE CH2 ...... 29 J3
  CHNE CH2 ...... 40 D5
Queensferry Industrial Estate
  CO CH5 ...... 26 C4
Queensferry Primary School
  CO CH5 ...... 26 A3
The Queens Lower School
  CH/BCN CH1 ...... 29 J4
Queens Park High School
  CHSW/BR CH4 ...... 3 F7
The Queens School
  CH/BCN CH1 ...... 2 C4
Ramada Hotel
  CHSE CH3 ...... 40 E2
Rector Drew Junior
  Aided School
  MOLD/BUCK CH7 ...... 36 B2
Rhescyoe Primary School
  HLYW CH8 ...... 11 F6
Rhosesmor Industrial Estate
  MOLD/BUCK CH7 ...... 22 A6
The Ridings Infant School
  CH/BCN CH1 ...... 18 B5
Rowton Hall Country
  House Hotel
  CHSE CH3 ...... 41 G5
Royal Chester Rowing Club
  CH/BCN CH1 ...... 3 G5
St Anthonys RC
  Primary School
  CHSW/BR CH4 ...... 38 E4
St Clares RC Primary School
  CHSW/BR CH4 ...... 39 G5
St Davids High School
  CHSW/BR CH4 ...... 38 C3
St Davids RC Primary School
  MOLD/BUCK CH7 ...... 43 G2
St Davids Trading Estate
  CHSW/BR CH4 ...... 38 D5
St Ethelwolds Primary School
  CO CH5 ...... 25 K4
St Martins Clinic
  CH/BCN CH1 ...... 2 D4
St Martins Gate
  CH/BCN CH1 ...... 2 C3
St Mary's Centre
  CH/BCN CH1 ...... 2 E6
St Marys RC Primary School
  FLINT CH6 ...... 13 H4
St Oswalds CE Aided
  Primary School
  CH/BCN CH1 ...... 18 E4
St Richard Gwyn Catholic
  High School
  FLINT CH6 ...... 13 H4
St Theresas Catholic
  Primary School
  CH/BCN CH1 ...... 29 F3
St Thomas of Canterbury
  Blue Coat CE Junior School
  CH/BCN CH1 ...... 2 C1
St Werburghs & St Columbas
  RC Primary School
  CHNE CH2 ...... 3 K1
St Winefride's RC
  Primary School
  HLYW CH8 ...... 7 K2
St Winefride's Well
  HLYW CH8 ...... 8 A2
Saltney Clinic
  CHSW/BR CH4 ...... 38 C4
Saltney Ferry Primary School
  CHSW/BR CH4 ...... 38 B4
Sandycroft Industrial Estate
  CO CH5 ...... 26 D5
Sandycroft Primary School
  CO CH5 ...... 26 C5
Saughall Thomas Wedge
  CE Junior School
  CH/BCN CH1 ...... 18 A5
Sealand Child Health Centre
  CO CH5 ...... 26 D1
Sealand Industrial Estate
  CH/BCN CH1 ...... 38 E1
Sealand Primary School
  CO CH5 ...... 26 C2

Shotton Infant School
  CO CH5 ...... 25 K2
Soughton Hall Hotel
  MOLD/BUCK CH7 ...... 33 H2
South Down Primary School
  MOLD/BUCK CH7 ...... 34 C5
Spencer Industrial Estate
  MOLD/BUCK CH7 ...... 35 F4
Stamford Gate Hotel
  HLYW CH8 ...... 8 B4
Sychdyn Primary School
  MOLD/BUCK CH7 ...... 33 G4
Taliesin Junior School
  CO CH5 ...... 25 J3
Tarvin Road Medical Centre
  CHSE CH3 ...... 3 K4
Travelodge
  HLYW CH8 ...... 22 B1
  MOLD/BUCK CH7 ...... 24 C5
University of Chester
  CH/BCN CH1 ...... 29 J5
Upton-by-Chester Golf Club
  CHNE CH2 ...... 29 K1
Upton-by-Chester High School
  CHNE CH2 ...... 30 B2
Upton Heath CE
  Primary School
  CHNE CH2 ...... 30 A1
Upton Westlea Primary School
  CHNE CH2 ...... 30 A2
Venerable Edward Morgan
  RC Primary School
  CO CH5 ...... 25 J3
Vicars Cross Golf Club
  CHSE CH3 ...... 31 J5
Victoria Infant School
  CH/BCN CH1 ...... 2 C1
Virgin Cinemas
  CH/BCN CH1 ...... 29 F5
The Watergate
  CH/BCN CH1 ...... 2 C5
Wats Dyke Infant School
  MOLD/BUCK CH7 ...... 34 A5
Waun-y-Llyn Country Park
  WRXW/BB LL1 ...... 50 D5
Waverton Community
  Primary School
  CHSE CH3 ...... 41 J5
Welsh College of Horticulture
  MOLD/BUCK CH7 ...... 23 F5
Wepre Park
  CO CH5 ...... 25 G4
Wepre Primary School
  CO CH5 ...... 25 F3
West Cheshire College
  CHSW/BR CH4 ...... 39 K3
Western Avenue
  Medical Centre
  CH/BCN CH1 ...... 28 D4
Westwood Primary School
  MOLD/BUCK CH7 ...... 34 D6
Woodfield Primary School
  CHNE CH2 ...... 30 C3
Wood Memorial CP School
  CHSW/BR CH4 ...... 38 E4
Ysgol Belmont
  MOLD/BUCK CH7 ...... 34 D4
Ysgol Bryn Gwalia CP
  MOLD/BUCK CH7 ...... 42 E3
Ysgol Croes Atti
  Primary School
  FLINT CH6 ...... 13 H3
Ysgol Delyn
  MOLD/BUCK CH7 ...... 43 F3
Ysgol Estyn
  WRX/GR/LL LL12 ...... 51 J5
Ysgol Gwenffrwd
  Primary School
  HLYW CH8 ...... 7 K2
Ysgol Maes Garmon
  MOLD/BUCK CH7 ...... 43 F4
Ysgol Maesglas
  HLYW CH8 ...... 5 G5
Ysgol Merllyn
  FLINT CH6 ...... 9 H5
Ysgol Owen Jones
  MOLD/BUCK CH7 ...... 23 G5
Ysgol Y Fron
  HLYW CH8 ...... 8 A3

Acknowledgements

Schools address data provided by Education Direct.

Petrol station information supplied by Johnsons.

Garden centre information provided by:

Garden Centre Association  Britains best garden centres

Wyevale Garden Centres

The statement on the front cover of this atlas is sourced, selected and quoted
from a reader comment and feedback form received in 2004